How to PITCH & PROMOTE Your Songs

FRED KOLLER

Writer's Digest Books

Cincinnati, Ohio

93 92 91 90 89 88   5 4 3 2 1

Library of Congress Cataloging-in-Publication Data

Koller, Fred, 1950-
  How to pitch and promote your songs.

  Includes index.
  1. Popular music—Writing and publishing. 2. Sound recording industry. I. Title.
MT67.K565 1988   784.5'0068'8   88-20769
ISBN 0-89879-323-8

Design by Clare Finney

Life is but a song.

CONTENTS

ACKNOWLEDGMENTS

I would especially like to thank all of the songwriters I have collaborated with over the years. Every writing session has been a learning experience. I would also like to thank the N.S.A.I. for their support of all songwriters at every level. It was at one of their seminars that I met Julie Wesling Whaley, editor of *Songwriter's Market,* who approached me with the concept for this book.

Finally, my thanks to Howard Wells of Wells & Associates, whose editorial assistance in organizing my rambling thoughts helped make this book readable, and to all the staff at Writer's Digest Books who work to keep inspiring writers and songwriters everywhere.

WHO IS FRED KOLLER
AND WHY SHOULD YOU READ HIS BOOK?

The question songwriters are asked most often—even than "What comes first, the words or the music?"—is "So you're a songwriter . . . What do you do for a living?" In publishing and recording centers like Nashville and Los Angeles, would-be songwriters can be found in almost any occupation *but* songwriting. They are all chasing a dream, believing they've got the special something that will make their talent stand out from the crowd. Like actors searching for the right agent who knows the right producer, songwriters search for the publisher who can get their songs recorded by the top acts and lead the way to membership in that select group of songwriters who are consistently on the charts. These songwriters know they can write songs as good as the ones on the radio but they don't understand the process of getting songs directly to the producer or artist.

There is no secret initiation or handshake among the elite of the music industry. The songwriters on the charts today got there through consistent hard work and an acquired knowledge of both the artists and the audience that the artists sing to. This book is for anyone who believes his or her songs are competitive and appropriate for a specific recording artist. It will also serve as a guide to self-publishing for those of you who are performers and want to record your own material.

I believe that a songwriter or publisher who devotes the same amount of time he'd use in trying to get someone else to mail tapes and make appointments in researching how to do it himself can be successful if HE HAS PROFESSIONAL MATERIAL AND A PROFESSIONAL PRESENTATION.

PROFESSIONAL PRESENTATION

With the right song almost anything is possible. Everybody loves a great song but too few people understand the songwriting and publishing processes. Too much of the general public assumes that the recording artist who makes a song popular is also the composer, because songwriters frequently aren't given proper credit. And too few composers believe they could successfully publish their songs, or at least copublish them, because they don't fully understand what publishing a song means. But you *can* pitch and promote your own songs. If you've got the right song for the right artist at the right time, anything is possible. Assuming that you've already written the right song, we can proceed. . . .

This book is about how I approach publishing and pitching songs every day. It will help you understand the various routes you can use to get your material to an artist or the artist's representative. This book is *not* a bible. Nothing is written in stone. No two songwriters have reached success by the same route. But every week somebody in every style of music is reaching the top of the charts, and almost always with a new song. Hopefully, one of those songs could be yours or mine.

Just a note about pronouns. The music industry—maybe even more than any other—has had superstars of both genders. Writing, performing, producing, and publishing songs has been done successfully by men as well as women. I've used pronouns like "he" or "she," simply for clarity.

WHO IS FRED KOLLER?

I've had a lot of different publishing experiences, from being a staff writer to copublishing to self-publishing. By sharing with you what I've been through and what I've learned, I hope to prepare you for some of what you'll encounter as you try to pitch and publish your songs.

In 1972 I was comanaging a small coffee house in Champaign-Urbana, Illinois. Dan Fogelberg and a couple of other acts were attending college there and performing regularly, and we got some fairly good out-of-town acts to play for the door.

I was an extremely weak vocalist/guitar player, but I played halfway decent dobro and bottleneck slide guitar, and often wound up sitting in with the acts that were coming through. It was here that I first encountered performers who were also trying to support themselves through songwriting. Even the local performers were composing their own songs and I decided to try my hand.

My first attempts were definitely amateurish novelty songs but other performers who only seemed to be capable of writing more "serious" songs were soon asking for lyrics and tapes so that they could add some humor to their acts. I wanted to play coffee houses and travel the country but was so insecure about my singing that even when I did "go on the road" it was as a back-up guitarist. I ended up very broke in upstate New York, disillusioned with the folk scene. I'd been sharing an apartment with a group of performers who had tried their hand at songwriting in Nashville. One morning, out of the blue, a royalty check came for one of them from BMI. The performer who received it told me that back when his songs were getting a lot of airplay he made a couple of thousand dollars every few months on a few recordings by other artists. It was like the old cartoon where the light goes on over the inventor's brain.

I spent the rest of the winter trying to write songs and finally had three that I thought were competitive with what I was hearing on the radio and in clubs. Singer/songwriters like Kris Kristofferson and John Prine were coming into vogue. My songs weren't country but they were closer to that style of music than rock and roll.

Nashville was the closest music center and I hitchhiked here on April Fool's day. After finding a place to stay, I went from publisher to publisher getting opinions on my songs. I'd had the good sense to get one of the better singers at the coffee house to demo them. Thanks to that, and the fact that I was willing to make some immediate changes, I was able to get a publisher to give me a small advance for the publisher's half of one of my songs. The door was opened and I began to learn all I could about professional songwriting. The small company that had taken my one song wasn't in a financial position to sign any staff writers to a weekly draw, so I attempted to support myself by performing in clubs and by living as frugally as possible. It was well over a year later that I was able to get another publisher to give me another small advance but I was getting to know my way around Music Row.

It was like being part of a freshman class in college or high school. You get to know who your peer group is and you learn to support each other by working together on songs and demos. With any luck these will be people you'll be working with for years to come. I finally got a staff writing contract for a ridiculously small amount of money and was able to get my first cuts.

I was hired because my songs had potential and I was an "idea" person. Through collaboration with other songwriters employed by that firm I was able to start getting some songs recorded. A lot of the initial ideas for the songs came from me but my lyrics were heavily edited by much more experienced writers at the firm who became my co-writers. The publishing company was a place to meet collaborators, and artists and producers were frequent guests at the office. When I wasn't busy trying to come up with new song ideas I was making a little extra money taping copies of the songs that the company was acquiring. It was a great learning experience to get to listen to hundreds of hits and songs that they'd published hoping to make into hits. I learned to detect different writers' trademark styles and could hear how demos had changed over the last fifteen years.

Before long, some of my songs were recorded. It's quite a thrill to hold a record with your name on it for the first time. Unfortunately it was some time later before I ever got to hear one of my songs on the radio. It seemed that the acts that were recording my songs all *used* to be famous. I was having songs recorded by Rosemary Clooney and The Sons of the Pioneers, but they weren't burning up the charts. After twenty or thirty of these types of covers I was extremely frustrated and left Nashville to work on my songwriting in a different environment.

Throughout this book I will stress the importance of research but it must be the right kind of research. I had spent too much time listening to the historical origins of country music. In retrospect I believe I went too far back in my research. My songs would have probably been hits in 1949 but this was the late seventies and the entire industry was moving towards a more "pop" sound that I didn't feel comfortable with. When I tried to write that type of song I felt like I was creating a parody instead of a topical song I could be proud of. So even with a number of records under my belt I knew that I would have to either wait for the industry to come around to where I was or try to change my style.

Frustrated, I moved to Santa Cruz, California and played in bands. Gradually I lost contact with the music business. Every now and then someone would record one of my songs but it was still the same syndrome.

I opened a used bookstore and read books all day long. After a couple of years of dealing with customers I was beginning to miss performing. I started teaching guitar which involved learning other writers' songs so that I could show someone else how to play them. Next I started writing songs rather than reading in the afternoons and after a few months there was almost always a guitar and a legal pad somewhere near the cash register. But I was writing country songs and the Santa Cruz musical community was not oriented that way. Lacy J. Dalton was a fellow starving folksinger and we would play each other our latest creations but there were no real outlets for material unless you performed them yourself. I still didn't believe I could sing my songs. But I did feel that the songs I wrote were pretty good. The frustration of feeling so close with the material I was creating but physically so far away from Nashville convinced me to sell my business and go back to Nashville.

This time I arrived with some money in my pocket and a better idea of what was necessary to get songs cut. It still took awhile to figure who was who and it was almost a year before I signed on as a staff writer again. Even though I had gotten songs recorded by many artists previously I was still caught up in the old system where the songwriter writes the song and collects the songwriter's share of the royalties and the publisher who signs the song pays for the demo and gives you some kind of advance or weekly draw in exchange for the publisher's share. The thought of asking for some of the publishing never crossed my mind. It was almost unheard of. Pop writers from Los Angeles had been getting pieces of their publishing for years and a few Nashville-based composers like Felice and Boudleaux Bryant had the foresight to be very creative in their publishing deals. It may have been a matter of the writers not knowing how much they were sharing until they started to make some decent royalties or it may have been the publishers never really explaining how the system worked.

In any case, I finally had a top ten record and then another one. The royalties were very nice. Back then, publishers with a chart record or an established catalog could go to their performing rights agency and get an interest-free advance. It wasn't really coming out of their own pockets—it was a loan, but you didn't have to have any more collateral than a chart record by a name artist. If you didn't quite pay them back on this record, one of the other songs you had added to your catalog while surviving on the advance money probably would put you in the black. They would often use this advance to pay their songwriters a draw or to create expensive demos.

One day everything changed. The advances were frozen while the industry awaited a Supreme Court decision. (The "Buffalo Broadcasting" decision dealt with blanket licensing of songs by BMI and ASCAP. It was brought by independent broadcasters after a similar suit by major broadcasters. If the independent stations had won, we as publishers would have to negotiate separately with thousands of stations that aired our songs.) Everyone had to wait for their royalties to come in. The advances have remained frozen and slowly the larger publishers with better cash flow have grabbed up the little companies. The company I worked for went from 24-track demos to a cassette porta-studio overnight but continued to receive the publisher's full 50 percent of the royalties. They maintained a full staff but you could definitely feel the pinch. I had another top ten record and when the time came to renew my contract I asked for a larger advance. In the old days the publisher would have called my performing rights agency and probably gotten the money from them based on my track record, but times had changed. I was doing most of my own pitching anyway and demos really didn't require a costly production to get cut if the songs were solid. The publisher was still receiving all of the publisher's share of royalties—a full 50 percent of my songs' income—but I was doing many of the publisher's duties myself. When my contract expired I went into business for myself.

At this point I was co-writing with a number of songwriters still affiliated with major publishers and I continued to get cuts. I banked some of those royalty checks and by not being frivolous was able to hang in there, no mean accomplishment. I recently co-wrote and copublished a number one country hit, "Goin' Gone," and have many other recordings coming out. For me it was learn by doing and it took a long time and a lot of hard work. I can't give you a magic shortcut, but I can teach you what I've learned about being a self-employed songwriter. Once you understand who does what in the music industry and learn how to research artists and trends, you will be ready to pitch and promote your songs.

TODAY'S MUSIC BUSINESS

As long as I've worked in the music business I can never remember hearing anyone say, "Gee, there sure are a lot of wonderful songs on the radio these days." It's easy to blame songwriters for the bad songs, or the lack of really great songs, and just as easy to point the finger at radio, record labels, producers, and artists. Or it's easy to just fault the publishers for not supporting songwriters who were "different from the norm." But before jumping to any conclusions you first have to understand just how the music industry looks at the songwriter.

THE PUBLISHER-SONGWRITER RELATIONSHIP

The music industry is a huge business that presents recordings of new and old songs to the public in the hopes that millions of copies will sell and everyone involved will make money. Songs are the heart of the business. Someone has to write them and someone has to publish them. The songwriter and publisher have traditionally had an employee/employer relationship. The music publisher's place in the music industry has been that of a silent partner who worked hand in hand with songwriters at every level of experience and shared equally in the financial rewards. A beginning songwriter would try to find a publisher to publish his songs in exchange for a certain percentage of the song's copyright. These percentages, usually 50/50 with the "writer's half" going to the songwriter and the "publisher's half" going to the publisher, were decided on by the publisher, who would "buy" them in exchange for providing demo recording facilities, and for presenting the songwriter's work to the music industry through contacts and experience. A songwriter would write a song and usually participate in the demoing. The publisher or his representatives would then show the song to record labels, artists, etc., until the song was either recorded or lost in the next wave of new songs. If your song was recorded, the record label would pay you for records sold and promote the record. Your performing rights agency would pay you for radio and television performances and everyone would come out smiling. Publishers hoped to develop long-term relationships with songwriters, and strong loyalties often resulted.

The beginning songwriter would start out on a song-by-song basis, and as some of the songs were recorded he or she would be offered the option of becoming a full-time staffer or exclusive writer at a salary recoupable from royalties. You paid your own way with copyrights, but as your copyrights improved and more people recorded your material your income improved as well. You didn't have to be a great singer or even a great musician. If you were a great lyricist you could become a professional songwriter through study and practice of the craft.

The publishers were often songwriters themselves and would work closely with the songwriter from initial idea to finished record. There were often tie-ins with record labels and many songwriters became successful recording acts. This was back in the days mentioned earlier, when publishers could get advances from the performing rights organizations.

Today, without those interest-free loans from BMI and ASCAP, publishers can't afford to develop beginning songwriters. If you are just starting out you had better be talented enough to also perform your own material or to somehow be able to support yourself as you learn the ropes.

Many publishers have discovered that songwriters who are also potential artists are their safest bet, simply because the publisher doesn't have to try to place the writer's songs with another artist. But, as many of these writers change publishers as often as they change record labels, the publisher—instead of being a salesperson out pitching songs—finds himself more in the role of a lobbyist, keeping track of their songwriter/artist's record label to make sure all the singles taken from the album are songs they have published, regardless of quality.

The old days of nurturing new songwriters are long gone and a non-artist songwriter may find a lot of doors closed. It is a very expensive proposition to take on a new writer, so publishers are hedging their bets by going only with proven writers and artists. I have to wonder, though, who they think will be providing new material in years to come.

SONGWRITERS AS PUBLISHERS

All songwriters share the goal of wanting to hear one of their compositions performed by an act with a large record-buying following. We've all dreamed of writing the song of the year or an anthem that will bring about an emotional response in the listener. Many songwriters would try to reach this goal by affiliating themselves with a strong publishing firm in the hopes that the publisher and his representatives could pave the way. After years of records that didn't make it all the way to the top, the frustrated songwriters realize that they could quite possibly achieve their goals just as quickly by publishing their own songs and serving as their own song plugger, secretary, accountant, and producer. If your publisher doesn't have the time or inclination to deal with you or no longer contributes the time and talent to deserve a full publisher's share, self-publishing is the most intelligent option. What does a publisher do? Can I do it myself? This book will answer those questions and also give you some insight into what a songwriter does day by day while trying to keep chart records coming.

The years of experience you get from being around a major publishing firm are invaluable, but you can write and publish and successfully pitch your own songs without ever working for one of the giants. You will have to be more than just a songwriter, though, so prepare yourself. The list of hats you can pile up on your head is limited only by your imagination. If you're going to self-publish, you'll have to be ready to work longer days and make every minute count. There'll be times when you want to co-write and you've already got the studio booked for a demo or you've got an appointment with an important producer that you shouldn't cancel. It can get pretty hectic. A staff songwriter or a songwriter who's supporting himself by freelancing one song here and another song there doesn't have to change hats so often. It's a quieter existence when you give your publishing to someone else. Most staff writers won't need to work with as many contacts throughout the industry as an independent songwriter because, presumably, the publisher is out there networking and promoting all the songs the writer signed over to him.

THE BENEFITS OF SELF-PUBLISHING

Why, then, should you try to publish and pitch your own songs? **You know your own catalog best.** Often, producers and artists are simply waiting for the right song to come along before they start in on their next album projects. The major publisher will have a large back catalog (plus songs created by their staff and picked up "off the street") to sort through before they make their pitch. They don't like to pitch large numbers of songs to any one artist so they'll usually take their two or three best pitches and move on to the next request. Those two or three songs could be yours or someone else's, the publisher may not really care. As an independent, you'll have the time and knowledge of your catalog to choose something appropriate from all the songs included in it. This doesn't mean that you should pitch more than two or three songs, but they'll be two or three songs that you have written and published. You'll just continue building your own catalog of copyrights that will grow in value as your songs become better known.

You don't have to follow industry dictates. The fact that no one will dictate what kind of song you should be writing is another important advantage to self-publishing. I write a lot of novelty songs which I've been pretty successful with, even though publishers had always asked me not to "waste my time on that silly stuff" when I could be using my talent elsewhere. As a self-published songwriter I can laugh a little louder when I hear one of those songs being performed.

The same holds true for any kind of writing that doesn't quite fit the industry norm. "Goin' Gone" was labeled "too folky" by more than one song publisher. I was lucky to hear about Nanci Griffith, an up-and-coming female vocalist on a small label who everyone said was "too folky," too. It doesn't take a college degree to guess who I pitched my song to first. The artist cut an excellent version of the song that attracted other acts to it, and a few years later I turned on the Sunday country chart countdown to hear that "Goin' Gone" was number one! I wish it was always that easy. But you always have to remember that the material must be strong enough to attract a number of cover versions including the one that goes all the way to the top.

You can choose your own collaborator. Another advantage of being your own publisher is being able to write with whomever you want. I co-wrote "Goin' Gone" with two writers who I knew very little about at the time. Some of my former publishers and song pluggers might have frowned on my writing with writers who weren't in-house and hadn't had top ten records. I wanted to work with new people and many of our collaborations have been recorded.

You can "target" your research. A lot of the major publishers don't have time to sit down and listen to each artist's individual album. They may have met with the producer and heard the songs he's already recorded for the new project, but it probably won't be that different from what has been done before. Everyone seems to have a trademark style. It's up to you to learn to spot them, and incorporate them in demos aimed directly at certain producers' artists. Once you get a song recorded, the door opens a little bit wider.

You can make as many pitches as you want. Most major publishers will pitch one copy of the song to the producer and let it go at that. If you believe strongly enough in your song being right for the artist, you can spend a few dollars more and pitch a tape to the artist's manager, record label, and whoever else could be a good contact until you know for certain that someone close to the artist has heard your song. This may take a little more time, but the payoff is worth it. Be competitive, but don't be pushy. If a tape comes back stamped "We Do Not Accept Unsolicited Material," try a different approach. Send a polite cover letter to the appropriate contact people asking permission to submit your best song. If they don't have time to listen to at least part of one song, they shouldn't be in the business. Believe it or not, they can tell after only a few seconds whether or not a song is suitable. *Always be as professional as possible.*

You control the bottom line. A publisher is always going to want to control as much of the publisher's share of the copyright as is available, to recoup his expenses. Publishers see every writer as someone who's been advanced so many dollars and earned back so many dollars. No matter how much they may like you as a person, they only see you in terms of the bottom line when you haven't had any covers in a while. For those of you who haven't worked with a major publisher, here's an example.

I write a song for you, the publisher. We sign a standard publishing agreement that gives me 100 percent of the writer's share and you 100 percent of the publisher's share. You like my material and offer me a $1,000 a month draw against royalties. I sign an exclusive songwriter's contract for two years and turn in forty songs a year. Halfway through the second year I co-write a top ten record with one of the other in-house writers. My performance royalties are $25,000 from BMI (as are my co-writer's), and you the publisher get $25,000 in performance royalties from my half and another $25,000 from my co-writer's half because both of us have signed away the publisher's share to you. This income is not recoupable against the draw you've been advancing me which is now up to $20,000. My draw is being paid back out of income from record sales and sheet music that has added up to only a few thousand dollars.

I still owe you on my draw, even though you've done quite nicely on the hit, not to mention the other songs I've also signed over to you. (Our draw situation is typical in that you get the publisher's share for the life of the copyright on all the songs I create during the time I'm a staff writer for your company.) If some of my other songs are also hits, I may actually break even on my draw, but the slow payments from record labels make it very hard unless I get a song on an album that goes platinum. For the songwriter/publisher, there's a lot more income once a song is recorded and released.

One disadvantage of self-publishing is that your songs will most likely be pitched to people through the mail. The major publisher will have someone on salary who has a personal relationship with the producer, artist, or label representative, and you won't. Don't let this scare you off. They are looking for the best song regardless of where it comes from. And if their artist doesn't record your song, another artist on another label probably will.

BECOMING AN INDEPENDENT SONGWRITER/PUBLISHER

The staff-writing situation described above is one where we'd both have to figure if it's really financially worthwhile to continue our partnership. Imagine that I've just had a hit and want a larger draw

6

but my draw is currently nowhere near being paid back. I realize that if I'd published the song myself I would still have gotten the cut and also be $25,000 richer. For that kind of money I could have paid myself the same draw and had enough left to have demoed my songs. Result: our current contract runs out and an independent publishing empire is born. As an independent, I want to be able to secure enough covers to keep the door open as I spend my savings trying to build a reputation for good songs. It's the same battle a staff songwriter faces but this time the war chest is coming out of my pocketbook. Many unknown songwriters feel that they have the material but can't seem to get a publisher interested enough to work with them. Eliminate the publisher and publish yourself. You'll be taking a risk but you'll stand to double your income if you are successful.

This book is aimed at independent songwriters working for themselves or small publishers trying to get their foot in the door. One of the keys to success in battle is knowing your "enemy" and being able to take advantage of his weak points. Your main competition for recordings will be from well-established staff writers who work for major publishers or, in some cases, for the producers themselves. Some producers rely so strongly on their own writing staff that pitching them songs is a waste of tape and time. (See "How to Read a Record Album," Chapter Four).

The majority of hits on the current country charts come from less than a hundred writers. The same familiar names keep popping up month after month, year after year. I know many writers with more than a dozen number one country hits who continue to get at least one top ten record every year. These writers will write as many as fifty songs a year and get a large percentage of those recorded. When they sit down to write it is often for a project that is already underway in which the producer has requested one of that writer's songs because he hasn't heard anything on the street that sounded like what he or the artist was looking for. This is your competition. Most producers go first to the major publishers and ask to hear all of the latest songs from this elite group of songwriters. Once you understand what their situation is like and how the system works, you will be able to pitch your songs more intelligently and actively compete for those chart positions.

THE PROS AND CONS OF STAFF WRITING

To compete with the big publishers and staff writers, you need to understand their situation. I worked as a staff writer for a number of major publishers for many years and my co-writing will still find me spending a day or two now and then down on Music Row watching the wheels go 'round. For the uninitiated here's what I've observed on the pros and cons of staff writing.

A publisher's office is a very strange environment for creativity but there are many successful writers who've learned to make it work to their advantage. A typical publisher's office will consist of a reception area where incoming calls and visitors are screened, an executive's office where songs are played for the more important producers and acts, and a couple of smaller offices that serve as writer's rooms. There will also usually be a room set aside for the publisher's catalog of songs and archives for recordings already secured where the tape copy person (usually an aspiring writer, too) makes up the tapes that are the publisher's livelihood. With the advent of low-cost multitrack studios and MIDI equipment, many publishers also devote an area of their offices to an in-house studio. Most of the staff writers have spent enough time around the major recording studios to be able to produce their own demos, and a large number of writers can also play an instrument well enough to perform on their own demos. The publisher will often let the writer sing his or her own lead vocals—many a deal has come about from a producer hearing the writer perform one of his own songs.

A typical day would go something like this:

The staff writer arrives in the morning and after coffee or whatever with the rest of the staff may be told that "Kenny" is looking for songs. The staff writer and a collaborator who may also be on staff write what they feel is a hit. These days many staff writers have their own studios at home so they may present the publisher or his assistant with a rough work tape that would probably not have much more than a lead vocal and a couple of other instruments. If the publisher likes what he hears he may suggest a certain feel or groove and have the writer book time in the in-house studio.

Here's where one of the first pitfalls of staff writing occurs. Most publishers will have at least four or five staff writers and a few freelance writers whose income isn't consistent enough to warrant being signed full time. When a big act that sells gold or platinum announces that he or she is looking for material, *all* of these writers will want to get into the in-house studio immediately. But there is a definite pecking order here. The established writers with the most hits can usually get the studio whenever they want. The new songwriters at the bottom of the ladder may often find themselves still waiting to get into the studio while every day "Kenny"—or whoever is looking—needs one less song. Every morning the song plugger makes his announcement, "Kenny doesn't want any more ballads" or "No more story songs for Kenny." Great songs can get lost in the wait for in-house studio time. You may ask: If the songwriter believes in the song that much, why doesn't he hire an outside studio? Well, he wouldn't want to pay for it himself—that's the publisher's job. The publisher may sometimes agree to such a measure but for the most part he figures that there will always be another golden opportunity to play the songs for Kenny's next album so why go to the expense? Pennies get pinched. It's a sad and frustrating situation to have your hands tied behind your back for a few hundred dollars' studio time, but it happens over and over again.

Even on a day-to-day basis, at a major publishing company with a large staff, the staff songwriters usually have to wait to make demos and often very good songs fall through the cracks. First the song will be presented in a simple voice-guitar or voice-piano arrangement to either the publisher or one of his assistants. Then they'll usually wait until the songwriter has four or five new songs and demo them as a group or, if the song is timely, they may try to tack it onto some other songwriter's demo. Most publishers tend to use the same musicians for all of their demos so don't be surprised if your song comes out sounding somewhat like every other tape that comes from that company. Even after you've demoed the song, the publisher's pitching staff will have to familiarize themselves with it, and precious time is wasted. But sometimes timing is just luck. There's always a chance that a producer will call just after you've finished a demo and your material, being at the top of the heap, will get cut.

If you're your own publisher, you don't have to stand in line to make a pitch or get studio time. If you can find a studio that has available time you can often do a demo the same day you wrote a song for an artist you heard was looking only hours before. You may even have purchased your own recording equipment to make simple demos at home. (This is something even writers for the major publishers are doing more and more because it's so incredibly frustrating to have a great song and no place to put it down.) Modern recording artists have to tour constantly to be able to afford their bands and staff. Managers want the act out on the road producing income. An act may fly in to Nashville on Wednesday and listen to songs on Thursday and then fly out to who knows where on Friday to perform. Even the best producers frequently go into the studio almost empty-handed, hoping that the act or the act's management has found some suitable material. Time and again I've heard of situations where the producer didn't like the songs the act found and vice versa. When you've got a studio and musicians booked for master sessions and no songs that "kill you" the word goes out and the song pluggers start to scramble. If you can create a song or re-demo one to fit an act in this type of situation, your odds of getting a cut are greatly enhanced.

To return to our "typical day" at the publishing house, I mentioned the song plugger was announcing the day's recording news. Sometimes the plugger is the secretary, sometimes it's the head of the company, and sometimes it's the tape copy person. Every publisher actively trying to get songs recorded will have at least one person who is in constant touch with who's looking for what kind of songs that week. The pluggers use tip sheets and phone calls and rumors on the street to figure out who's recording next. As an independent writer you may have to work a little harder at finding out exactly who's cutting when, but by learning to read a record album and concentrating on certain artists who will best fit your material, you can be remarkably accurate in predicting when someone is ready to go into the studio. You may actually have an advantage over the staff songwriter here, as the major publishers have too many people to keep informed. Unless a producer requests a certain writer's songs, the lowly songwriter who just started on the staff will often never know who's been looking for material.

THE LAST-MINUTE PITCH

What happens a lot is this. It's 5:30 on a Friday evening when Producer A has his secretary call over to the major publisher because the label or the artist has passed on the material he's already found, he's going to Vegas for the weekend, and wants a tape within the hour. If the song plugger has already headed for home or a bar, it falls into the hands of the secretary or tape copy person to make a tape containing the publisher's best songs. The "best" songs will almost always be the songs that were demoed the most recently. There may have been older songs perfect for the producer and the act but the parties responsible for this pitch weren't aware of them. It's a problem of shelf life, but more on that later.

The artist himself will be looking for twelve or fourteen hit songs to record for his next album. He may have one or two songs he's gotten from personal friends, friends of the band, or through his attorney or booking agent. When the time comes to find new material, no stone is left unturned. The producer will have gone around to various publishers and chosen another half dozen songs. There will probably be a large cardboard box of unsolicited material on the floor. Some of these tapes will be from major publishers, but others might well be yours and mine.

The first person to listen to these tapes will immediately eliminate the ones that are obviously from nonprofessionals. How do they know, you ask? I have seen too many situations where someone has sent ten songs on a cassette that looked like it had been in constant circulation since the early sixties. The titles are written in ball-point pen with the previous title still showing through. There might even be some tape holding the anti-record holes together! Don't let your song be eliminated on the basis of a sloppy demo package. Professionalism isn't that expensive.

Last-minute pitches are exciting, but will probably be an uncommon occurrence for most independent publishers. The main reason is that the record labels are like most of us. When we go shopping we usually go first to the biggest store and hope that they'll have what we need among the thousands of items available. The labels and producers start at the biggest publishing companies but like anyone who shops at the little specialty stores or by mail order, they may also remember that little "store" that always had quality material one couldn't normally find. As an independent publisher, you're trying to create a catalog of excellent songs that can be pitched at any point and will reflect the overall quality of your catalog.

FROM SONGWRITER TO PUBLISHER

Every week a new batch of songwriters moves to a music business center like Nashville or Los Angeles, hoping for immediate success. They may have saved up some money to support themselves for a while, and/or intend to continue working at another occupation while knocking on doors looking for a publisher who will point them down the yellow brick road.

Almost every beginning writer I encounter believes that a publisher is the key to success and riches. They've all heard how songwriters like Don Schlitz (who wrote "The Gambler") breezed into town and seemed to be overnight sensations but they ignore the fact that Don's song was published by a very small company run by a record producer and another songwriter, Paul Craft. Don already had the key ingredient to success—a great song—and like myself and all the other new songwriters probably didn't believe that it was possible to get your songs recorded without a powerful publisher's assistance.

SETTING GOALS

It's impossible to say that if you follow a particular set of rules you'll achieve your goal in a given period of time. The wonderful thing about the music industry is the constant need for something new. An excellent short-term goal for every beginner should be an understanding of the music system. Many musicians who've played the road or worked at a club in their own hometowns don't really understand how artists and producers go about selecting the material they record. To them, it's all some huge, unknowable, political machine that makes millions of dollars. So they send tapes to publishers when they're feeling brave but even that's scary because they all know of some guy or girl with a lot of talent who was rejected by Nashville or Los Angeles and wound up never writing another song. We've all heard this song and dance more times than we need to.

If your songs are strong enough and you work at pursuing a songwriting career you will be discovered. Recording artists won't come looking for you, though. You have to make the initial approach and you should know what can or can't be done. I can tell you your song is a hit and you can agree, but we need to find a recording artist if we want to test the market and see what we've got. Instead of looking for immediate or easy success, songwriters should develop a step-by-step plan, or at least a strategy, for their career.

A major priority, then, is learning who the players are. Too many people try to bluff their way through the music business. Don't be one of them. Read the trade publications like *Billboard* and *R&R*. Go down to the corner market and look through the magazines devoted to today's song hits. You need to know who's doing what. When someone asks you who you hear performing one of your songs, have an answer ready for them. Your own enthusiasm for your songs is contagious. The songwriter who's walking around defeated is his own worst enemy. If your songs aren't getting better and better, go back and figure out where you slipped off the track.

Once you know who the players are, one of your main goals should be to get one of your songs recorded. It is not an impossible goal if approached in the proper fashion.

Any act that isn't firmly established as a constant money-maker is a good prospect for a beginning songwriter's songs. I know of many cases where songwriters didn't want their best songs pitched to artists they considered unknowns or on the way down. This can be a mistake. Your other main goal should be to get your songs out on the street so people can hear them. The first artists to record my songs were acts who had had very successful careers but had fallen from the public eye and were hoping for a comeback. Artists of this type are much more likely to take what they hear as a hit song from a non-established songwriter. The "hot" songwriters will probably already have all of their best material on "hold" with the best-selling acts (more on that later) and producers and the professional song pluggers often ignore acts on the comeback trail. This also holds true for new acts just recording their first album or changing over from one style of music to another.

I recently had a song recorded by an "unknown" folksinger on a small folk label. Before her album was released a well-known producer heard her version and one of his artists who had had a string of hits a few years back recorded it. The same version was also heard by three other acts, two of which were among the hot newcomers. One of those acts has since recorded the song and it's been taken into the studio by two others. A publisher was not involved. It was just a good song that someone heard on a reasonably obscure record.

A songwriter who's left another career to pursue songwriting on a full-time basis often has initial goals that get even more specialized. You need to be able to give yourself day-to-day or week-to-week goals to keep letting yourself know that you're not spinning your wheels. John Prine was so excited about learning a new chord to add to the few chords he already knew that he wrote a wonderful song entitled "Hello in There" that incorporated the new chord throughout the song. Progress was being made.

Before you visit the major music centers you'll want to overcome any fear of performing your songs for others and develop a thick skin to accept the fact that not everyone is that interested in the song you wrote about your girlfriend's dimples. It's hard to have someone you've never met before critique the song you've been working on for a month and a half. Often as not, if you're still just beginning, such a critique will suggest changes that will radically alter your song. It takes a while to learn how much you'll bend.

After getting past the fear of harsh criticism from the people who screen and select material, you need to be ready to turn your songs over to total strangers to perform. Every performer will want to inject his own ideas on how to interpret your song, and once again you need to learn to accept the good with the bad. I've written songs for certain acts and had them look at me like I was out of my mind but I've learned to be flexible. No two people have the same taste. And it would be mighty boring if we did. Once you've gotten to the point where you tell people that you're a songwriter and then follow through by presenting them your creation, you've come to meet the MUSIC BUSINESS face to face.

SETTING UP THE PITCH

This is a very easy occupation to get cynical and bitter about. You work and work on a song until you think it's perfect. You've recorded your demo within the limits of your budget and now it's time to try and show off your new masterpiece. A professional attitude will make or break you at this point. Here's an example of a situation I see over and over again:

A songwriter has just written what he feels is a perfect song for a current best-selling act. He calls the act's record label and is told to drop off a tape. Drop off a tape!! This is priority material and the songwriter wants an answer that day, or at least within the week. Often as not, the songwriter gives up then and there, telling himself that no one's going to listen to his humble tape.

Sometimes he may get lucky and be allowed to sit down with the A&R (artist and repertoire) person at the label or the producer's assistant. If you get an appointment, you need to know in advance who's who. You should already have a mental list of the various acts on the label who could possibly record the song, and if the pitch is being made to the producer or manager you should know which recording artists they're currently involved with. Better still, find out what their past track record is and mention the fact that you enjoyed a record they produced a couple of years back. (But if you're talking with the label rep and his main act just bombed on their last three singles, don't mention how well they're doing.)

Major publishers can get so wrapped up in acquiring catalogs that they lose touch with who's up and coming. As an independent publisher, you will have a major advantage here. By focusing on a few acts who might record your material and by having fewer (but hopefully better) contacts than a big publisher, you will be better able to keep up with what's going on in these people's careers. The key is singling out acts that will be receptive to your material and studying their careers until you make a breakthrough. You can pleasantly surprise the professional you're meeting by showing that you've taken an interest in his career. Let the people you meet with know just how actively involved you are with the recording industry. Getting drunk with some act's drummer in a local musicians' hangout is not the key to success. Learn as much as you can before you send a tape out and be even better prepared when meeting with someone in person. This is a very people-oriented industry so let them know that you're paying attention. If you don't know, ask.

GETTING PAST THE SECRETARY'S DESK

It's easy to spot the beginning songwriter who has finally gotten past the receptionist at a publishing house or record label. You can tell by the way he holds his head up high as he's summoned to the publisher's assistant's office that a threshold has been crossed in every sense of the word. After months of being asked to "Please leave a tape," at long last he's being summoned into the inner sanctum.

Amazingly enough, though, once he gets there, it looks a lot like a midwestern insurance office, with workers busy filling out forms and filing things away while the songwriters are gathered in their cubicles trying to get the creative wheels turning. In other offices copies of demonstration tapes are being made to be delivered to various record labels and producers and a visiting artist or producer might be around to add a small degree of excitement to the proceedings.

The person screening songs will probably make some small talk about the weather or whatever and then ask you for your tape. Here's an opportunity for your research to pay off. If you're going to see Jack Black at XYZ Records or Publishing Company you will want to have done your homework and know a little about this person and his company. You may have just flown in for one day from Nowhere, Minnesota, but you should have taken time to do some homework. What songs does the label have on the charts. Get out that *Billboard* and read it on the plane or in the waiting room. Knowing that a hot act just bombed may keep you from saying something like, "Gee, the Bozo Brothers are sure doing swell." Don't be unprepared. Jack will wonder what rock you've been under if you don't know what's happening. If the label has a currently successful single you can let them know that you, too, are following its progress. Often as not, Jack Black may have had success himself as either a songwriter or producer. As a record collector, I will often be able to really break the ice by mentioning that Jack was the guitar player on one of my favorite old recordings. You've got to make sure they know that you're serious about your music and that you

16

KNOW WHEN TO MAKE AN APPOINTMENT

If you live a distance from a major music center like Los Angeles or Nashville, you should try to visit at least a few times a year if you can, to make contact with people face-to-face.

Wednesday afternoon is a great day for your business meeting. It's the middle of the week and everyone will be clear headed. (Everybody's heard about cars that are made on a Monday. It's the same for the music industry.) People need a little time to get back into the swing of things. The Friday afternoon before a major holiday is also a bad time to make an appointment. A lot of neophyte songwriters plan to come to a music center during Grammy week, or some other awards time. Sure, there's lots of excitement around town but no one has time to do anything. All the music offices around the country generally send their top people to town for important meetings and there are major industry awards banquets every night. You can't expect to get the attention you deserve at a time like that. Plan your visit so you can have an unhurried appointment.

Don't try to see three or four different labels or publishers in the same day. They don't like being played against one another and they might resent it if they thought you were "shopping around." I have made great contacts and gotten songs recorded when a two o'clock appointment ran well into the evening after I started playing some of my more unusual material.

When you make an appointment, be punctual even if the party you're seeing is usually late. I like to arrive fifteen minutes early so that I can sit and listen to what's going on. Record labels and managers will also have a wide selection of specialized music magazines that you may not subscribe to, so you can read up on the latest news while you're waiting. If the receptionist isn't swamped, find out how the act's latest record is doing.

The receptionist or secretary at most offices knows exactly what's going on, and can be an important ally. Everything goes through her. I have seen more than one songwriter try to push past the secretary or try to impress her with an air of self-importance. Be friendly and positive. Leave her glad you came by. Remember the receptionist's name and use it the next time you call.

The professionals you'll deal with expect you to be able to make a presentation of your songs that was worthy of their time. If they don't like your material it isn't their job to tell you who might. If they do like your material and ask for revisions, they expect these revisions will be done in the next few days.

17

have and can do your research to come up with the best possible material for their projects.

Etiquette is often sorely lacking and your patience will be tried every step of the way. Nothing happens fast; every part of the process seems to involve three or four decisions by people who like to take forever. But it's worth the wait when you're out on the road someplace far from home and hear one of your songs on the radio.

PART-TIME/FULL-TIME SONGWRITING

I've been very lucky in being able to have supported myself as a songwriter for the past fifteen years without having to do anything but write and perform songs and speak at songwriting seminars. I haven't had to get a "day job." This is not due to any great success but to a frugal lifestyle and a firm conviction that if I had to be a bartender or whatever I could do it in a much more beautiful place than those cities chosen to be music capitals.

The recording centers grew up around the big radio shows and movie capitals. They've become a big business. Music Row in Nashville, once a quaint neighborhood, is bristling with multistory office buildings. If you ask a waiter or waitress there what he or she does in their spare time they likely as not tell you that they're working at being a songwriter.

If you're going to make the commitment and move to a place like Nashville, L.A., or New York to be a songwriter, make sure that any other career you have won't conflict. The music industry operates from 10 to 5 Monday through Friday, with studio sessions and showcases of songwriters and new acts often taking place two or three evenings a week. There's always some place to be seen and heard.

Many of today's successful songwriters started out as waitresses and waiters. They supported their craft until their songs started to get covered. Always strive toward that day when you can devote all of your time to your craft. You can be a part-time songwriter but make sure that you have time to do your music business during normal business hours. Once you're established as a songwriter it becomes even rougher to have two careers. It's perfectly all right for someone climbing the ladder to be a waiter/songwriter. But once you've established a reputation as a songwriter and are spotted working at another occupation the word seems to get around that you've given up songwriting (unless you have a cover story, like the I.R.S. wants a lot of money tomorrow or whatever). The one acceptable co-occupation for a songwriter seems to be real estate agent. When I asked some of my songwriter/realtor friends why, they said that the public perceives each occupation as one that requires little time or talent. So it goes . . .

FULL-TIME SONGWRITING

As a full-time songwriter you soon learn that there is never a free moment. At three in the morning, while you're on vacation, an idea will come to you for a song. That song may or may not pay the rent! So you get out of bed, find a pen and paper, and write it down. You also listen to strangers' conversations, TV shows, and try to read as many books, magazines and publications as possible for new themes, catch phrases, possible titles. Thinking you're going to remember an idea is just that—wishful thinking. Write it down! I've written some of my best songs on trains racing across the country while my fellow passengers snored into the night.

Not everyone is cut out for this lifestyle. You need to be able to work on one style of song in the morning with one collaborator and another totally different form of music in the afternoon. You also need to know when *not* to write. There will be days when it's better to wash the car. Songs are very delicate things, and trying to force them can make the end result sound superficial.

A full-time songwriter doesn't take weekends off. When you listen to the radio you are trying to match your catalog with the acts you're hearing. The record store becomes a reference library, and you are always trying to find ways to expose your songs to new acts.

We all have different work habits. Some of us will only write ten or twelve songs a year, but that doesn't mean that we weren't trying to come up with another hit 365 days out of the year. I know of one songwriter who buys four or five guitars a year, claiming that each instrument brings out a different song. He spends more time in guitar shops than most songwriters do in the studio but he produces excellent songs.

As a full-time songwriter, your friends, neighbors, and relatives will barrage you with "sure hit" ideas that "can't miss." Everyone thinks he can write a song. It looks easy, but you only get twenty or so lines to tell an entire story that people will want to hear over and over again. That is, at most, three minutes of fun and excitement, and you'd better make every second count.

What the publishers and record labels are looking for in those three minutes is a different viewpoint on common situations, a strong melodic sense, and an ability to make the words sound natural. In this day of MIDI-keyboards and home multitrack studios, a lyricist need not look far for work. You could easily establish yourself and spend month after month traveling the country collaborating. It's good to travel and stay in touch with the rest of the country outside of the music capitals. Many songwriters travel as far as Europe and Japan seeking collaborators.

I meet too many songwriters who are totally unfamiliar with any kind of music outside the genre that they're most interested in. You should always expose yourself to other outside influences to stay ahead of the pack. It's possible that one day someone from a style you haven't been paying that much attention to will want to collaborate.

You don't have to go out and buy every heavy metal album made, but it doesn't hurt to watch programs such as MTV for a couple of hours a month. All recording artists need good sounds, no matter what style of music they do. Writers of the heavy metal anthems are getting six-figure checks! You can bet that they see music and songwriting as a full-time occupation.

I would assume that every songwriter wishes he could give 100 percent to it. Always make sure your songs get that kind of effort.

SONGWRITER AND PUBLISHER

Being a songwriter/publisher definitely has its advantages, but you really have to ask yourself if the quality of your songwriting will be affected by the decision to publish your own songs. Don't get so caught up in the trappings of the business that you lose sight of your craft. Many songwriters waste a lot of time and money trying to *look* like major publishers when they should be working out of their home or car until that first really good record comes along. I would drop by their new office to see if they wanted to write a song and they'd be up a ladder hanging wallpaper, painting the window trim, or moving recently purchased furniture up and down a flight of stairs. After a couple of months of carpentry, moving, etc., they'd spent their savings, were buried in bills, and hadn't found the time to write songs to take into the studio to demo. Their dreams of self-publishing were soon over. Luckily, they got another staff writing job at another publisher.

What went wrong? To have an expensively appointed office with copy machines and computers (not to mention a staff) you have to have a sizable catalog that is consistently producing revenue. It may take a while to realize any income, and you may have to survive on your own savings.

Some songwriters have found investors who always wanted to be in the music business and were happy to loan some money to such an exciting project, but once again these writers were quickly caught up in the interior decoration business. To make matters worse, rather than having a publisher or song plugger with years of experience call to suggest that so-and-so was looking for material, they'd get a call from the investor at three in the morning on a Sunday suggesting that they ought to write a tune for the latest superstar. As if it hadn't crossed their mind! I'm sure that there are intelligent investors to successfully back your publishing venture, but I would recommend that he or she is made aware of the unpredictable nature of this business.

BEING INDEPENDENT IS TIME-CONSUMING

Even if you have the right attitude, it's difficult to be a songwriter and a publisher because of the time required for each. No two days are the same. One day you may be a songwriter in the morning and a recording artist at night. The next morning you may be a research librarian and that afternoon a song plugger. Just trying to find time to listen to the radio becomes a chore. Cassettes are everywhere. There will be weeks when you only come home to sleep and weeks when you never seem to leave the room where you do your writing. With the advent of home demos your only contact with the outside world may seem to be the pizza guy who brings sustenance every now and then.

Songwriting and publishing can be done anywhere in the world with the right amount of research and postage. But the closer you are to the source, the quicker new information will reach you. You won't learn that artist A needs one more up-tempo song unless you happen to know one of the musicians on the sessions or have an inside contact who trusts you to be able to come up with the right song. All of that comes with time.

If you've got the right songs and are intelligent and systematic about your approaches you should be able to get your foot in the door from anywhere. It happens every day. Look at any record store to see how many new albums come out within a year, a month, a week. Somebody's writing the songs, somebody's publishing them, and hopefully, somebody's buying them. All of this may seem trivial but it makes an important point, because it is at this stage that your lack of experience is most evident. Your contact with the recording artist, or those channels that directly lead to the recording artist, will likely be through the mail and if you play your cards right, they'll have no way of knowing if the tape is coming from a million-dollar corporation or a desk in some starving songwriter's apartment.

IS SELF-PUBLISHING FOR YOU?

How many times has your phone been cut off in the past year because you didn't pay the bill? How many late charges have you paid at the local video rental shop? When did you last write a letter or postcard? Do you hire help or rely on your companions when it's time to plan a party? Are you habitually late? Does your car look like you're holding a paper drive? Silly questions to some of us, but to some an ongoing nightmare.

If you are not used to planning and organizing and doing paperwork on an almost daily basis you had better think twice about self-publishing. It's not an easy occupation and as you get busier and busier as a songwriter or performer you'll come to wish you'd never started. You lie in bed worrying that your co-writers may not pay you for the last demos unless you send them an itemized bill, you lost all the receipts a month ago, and your cancelled checks might be somewhere in the car. Don't get into self-publishing without carefully considering the amount of time it will take. It's not hours every day, but it will be hours every week, and you will have to be constantly changing hats to think first like a songwriter, and then like a publisher.

As a publisher, you'll need to be objective about your work. Each songwriter thinks that his latest song would be perfect for artist A. A publisher will also know that artist A has already released three singles off of her latest album and just became a Buddhist. As your own publisher, you must be prepared to become much more analytical of your own work and that of others. It becomes a lot more competitive and every clue counts. There are still twelve or fewer cuts on any given album and you need to be constantly aware of those records your songs might fit on.

Don't let all of the above discourage you. By carefully planning your time and working a little earlier or later you can make it work. On a typical working day, I get up earlier than I did when I was still playing clubs and try to get all the correspondence I didn't finish the night before ready for my daily trip to the P.O. box, which serves as my "corporate headquarters." It's in a very impressive building with a nice flagpole out front, and the clerks have gotten used to my sending tapes to the far corners of the world.

If I'm not going to be in the studio doing some sort of demo I will probably have another hour to work on paperwork before I sit down to write new songs, either alone or in collaboration with others. I try to have at least one or two song titles or a new melodic idea ready before my collaborator arrives. Being more of a lyricist, I will often help my co-writers who are stuck with where to go with a song or, if a title strikes me right, I may try out a new set of verses with their completed melody and chorus. I try to get at least a rough draft finished before we quit for the day and then set another meeting for a week later to get back together and polish the song.

There will be subsequent meetings where we will discuss the demo: whose studio we'll use, who will sing what song, whether there will be a male and female version of the song, what artist we're directing the song to, etc. In and around all of this, we try to find the time to listen to the radio and hear what the public seems to like and to do research into various acts. As I've already mentioned, you need to know if an act you're pitching songs to is going up or down the charts or is even on the charts at all and also if this is the first or the last single of their current album. The research will keep you as busy as you want to be once you get rolling. There's an infinite number of places to sell your material. No one but you is responsible to see that it gets to the right party at the right time.

23

RESPONSIBILITY AND DISCIPLINE

I conduct seminars for songwriters' groups all across the country and will often suggest that a participant send a song I've critiqued to a certain recording artist. These seminars will usually be two-day affairs during which I ask the writer to get a copy of the artist's latest album and show them where to look for the best channels to the recording act. I try to create situations where I can return in four to six months to see what kind of progress is being made, listen to rewrites, and encourage improvements.

When I ask many of these would-be writers if they ever heard back from so-and-so about the song I suggested they pitch, the answer will invariably be "No." This is usually followed by some lame excuse like: "The song needs a new demo," or "My cassette deck is broken," or "I lost the address." By this time, the act I had initially suggested has usually finished the album he or she was working on and a song will get lost in a pile on someone's desk. If you want to be a successful self-published songwriter, there'll be no room for excuses. Besides wearing the hats of songwriter or publisher, you need to hone your skills as a producer and be able to create as professional a demo as possible within your budget. You'll also have to be an all-around businessperson. You'll type the lyrics, and write the letter asking permission to pitch your song. You'll also make the tape copy and see it's mailed off to the right address.

Even great songs sometimes need to be recorded over and over before somebody does a version that sets the world on its ear. You can't stop believing in your songs. Large publishers receive so much new material, even the best songs may get lost on the shelf. You have to discipline yourself to create more material without stopping and waiting for the industry to hear what you've already done. Some songwriters become so popular that all the record labels and producers seek out their old material to capitalize on their current popularity. Of course this phenomenon seldom lasts for more than a couple of years and only happens to a very lucky few. Last year's "songwriter of the year" can spend frustrating months wondering how his material changed, when all along it was the public's taste and the cycle always comes back around. The main thing to strive for is originality. Never give in to the urge to write a song that's not you for some "fast" money.

THREE

YOUR LOW-BUDGET PUBLISHING EMPIRE

What you call your company is an important consideration and getting to choose the name of your newly-founded publishing company is one of its initial perks. Both BMI and ASCAP have forms that you must submit for approval of your new company's name. It's a good idea to have at least three different names ready so you have an alternative if someone has already used your first choice. Many writers simply name the company after themselves, but here's a chance to show some originality to the person screening songs before he or she even listens to your tape. My own publishing company is called Lucrative Music, and I'm still surprised that no one else had thought of such an obvious name. I've seen some wonderfully personal names for publishing companies. Once again, it's a way to let the producers, artists, and managers you're pitching your songs to know what type of material to expect.

Songwriter/author Shel Silverstein hasn't suffered from calling his company Evil Eye Music. The name fits the humorous side of his songwriting talents. You just might get the attention of the secretary or assistant screening tapes by having a name that makes that person wonder what kind of songs you publish. It all comes down to whether or not your material is recordable.

SOME LEGAL PAPERWORK

In some areas of this country you may have to run a fictitious business name statement to be legal. You may also have to apply for a tax number if you plan on reselling cassettes or records or even your own sheet music. It varies a lot from state to state but a quick call down to the nearest Secretary of State's office should let you know what's required in your hometown.

BMI and ASCAP both do "worldwide" searches before granting you permission to use the name you have selected for your publishing company. But they only cover the use of that name as a publishing company. If the name was applicable, someone could possibly open a music store in your area with the same name as your publishing firm. A fictitious business statement will protect you from such an event. Consult knowledgeable individuals who understand the music business and the laws governing small business in your home state. Your local banker may be a good place to start. They have to deal with new businesses every day.

GETTING STARTED

One of the advantages to self-publishing is the relatively low cost of basic supplies. As I mentioned earlier, a common mistake of songwriters attempting to start their own publishing company is to go overboard with office supplies and equipment. Songwriter/performer John Prine was once asked what it takes to establish your own record label. He explained to the questioner that "You should go forty miles into the desert and find a large rock, place both hands on the rock and state 'I AM A RECORD LABEL.' " This may seem a bit sacrilegious, but the same procedure will work for starting your own publishing company. If you don't have a nearby desert and rock, the kitchen table will do.

Let's assume that you are not contracted to another publisher as a staff writer, but that you have written some songs that you feel will be competitive. Hang out your shingle! Most new businesses cost thousands of dollars just to open the door but it doesn't cost all that much to become a publisher. As an independent songwriter you will probably wind up working out of your home until your catalog generates enough income to afford office space. Your main concern as an independent is to make sure that your presentation is on the same quality level as any of the major publishers. Don't have someone doubting the quality of your songs before they've even listened to your material. It really doesn't cost much to look like a pro. One can easily get by with a few basic supplies.

BASIC SUPPLIES

Get the best typewriter you can afford. It's important that your cassette labels and lyric sheets look as professional as possible. It only takes a few seconds to type them out properly.

You may also want to spend an extra hundred dollars and have a graphic artist design a logo for your company. The added visual impact of your own logo on letterhead, envelopes, cassette labels, and your own business cards makes it an expense well worth considering.

Another inexpensive but professional-looking idea is to use your logo on the mailers in which you send your demo cassettes out. You can get by with a cleanly typed presentation until you feel you can afford this expense. I was surprised at how quickly I went through my first five hundred business cards. When I first started sending out cassettes I would include a business card in the cassette case so that the listener would have no excuse for not knowing who to contact. Whenever I got out to clubs and liked what the performers were doing I made sure they got one of my cards rather than a scrawled name on a napkin.

A phone answering machine is another essential item. You never know when a publisher, producer, or artist will call you for material.

If you have substantial savings, buy a computer and use it not only to keep track of all of the songs in your catalog, but also to help in your pitches. There already are some software programs aimed directly at publishers and songwriters. These programs are designed for calculating royalties, and will also help you keep track of income from various sources. If you already have a computer I would suggest that you check through magazines such as *Contemporary Keyboard* or those aimed at your own model of computer for these products.

I travel with an inexpensive tape recorder so that any ideas that come to me while driving can be put down on tape without pulling off the road. I've written more than one song this way. I've also collaborated on many songs that were initially scribbled on someone's bank deposit slip or whatever scrap of paper was handy. I no longer trust my memory. I like to write things down.

HOME OFFICE

A home office is a good place to start out as a publisher/songwriter. Home offices have long been an acceptable deduction from the I.R.S., provided you can substantiate the need for one and follow the sometimes confusing guidelines. Check with your local I.R.S. office for current regulations. They want you to set aside a separate area only for business purposes, but that percentage of your mortgage or rent payments can be considered a business expense.

Luckily for songwriters, all you really need is a comfortable place to sit and a couple of legal pads. Some songwriters have state-of-the-art keyboard equipment and a home studio setup that rivals the majors, but a good song can be created anywhere.

Let your neighbors know what you're doing. Tell them that strange people with bad haircuts and no visible means of support may be showing up at your house at odd hours. I've known of more than one songwriter whose neighbors thought he was engaged in some illegal activity. Once they knew what he did for a living, everything was fine. They even brought him ideas for songs. One of my neighbors once informed me that some musicians had moved in across the street. I asked him how he knew. He said the group's appearance was the tipoff—"a bunch of fat guys with skinny girls." Songwriters don't fare much better in the public's perception.

BANK ACCOUNTS

You've got yourself some good-looking letterhead and cassette labels. Your lyrics are neatly typed out and you've told a producer that you'd drop a tape off soon for the acts he's looking for. Now's the time to go to your local bank and open an account for your new publishing firm.

It will only take a couple of minutes to set up a separate account for your new publishing company once you've gotten the name approved by your performing rights organization (BMI, ASCAP, or SESAC). Getting to know your banker can pay off in the long run. If you're operating in a music center like Nashville, the bank is probably used to working with music industry people.

The local bank where you got your car loan or credit cards is a great place to start. Personnel there can guide you through the paperwork and possibly arrange a loan in the future, after you've established a relationship as a reputable businessperson.

If you've never been in business before, a visit to your local library or bookstore would be a good idea. The how-to/business section should have many books on running a small business and you can probably find one that will help you get started. An afternoon with an accountant who's familiar with the music business might also be money well spent. A good administrator can be very handy at this point.

Always think in terms of the future. The songs you're pitching today may be the first songs of yours a producer will hear. Let him associate your name with quality. It doesn't matter if the records that result are B-sides and album cuts as long as the songs stand out. Eventually you'll start to get those singles you need to survive.

It's a long haul unless you can get a major artist to record one of your songs almost as soon as you open your door for business, and even that's no guarantee of instant riches. If you wrote a number one hit song today it would be at least a year to two years before it would generate any income except for advances or loans against advances. The performing rights organizations no longer give advances, but they will work with your banker on guaranteeing a loan after you've had chart success. It's a financial fact we all have to consider.

NOW YOU'RE IN BUSINESS

I've already talked about how important your visual presentation to the record labels, artists, and producers must be. A small investment with a designer can pay for itself the first time your tape gets taken home because they like your logo. I can't stress enough how important professionalism is so I will repeat this thought again and again in these pages. Behind the scenes your company can look like a college dorm room but with a little organization it can present a businesslike face to the world.

All of these details add up and help build the proper image for your company. Too many fly-by-night publishers are currently out on the streets acting unprofessional. You need to put as much distance as you can between these individuals and yourself. The producers and artists listening to your songs generally hope for the best but expect the worst. They will probably listen to the most accessible (professionally packaged) tapes from well-known publishers first. Your demo doesn't have to be elaborate, but it does have to be competitive.

You will need two professional-quality tape decks to make copies from one to another. Those "boom box" stereos aren't made for all-day, every day abuse, and spending a little more money early on is a wise decision. You can use a cassette-to-cassette system, but most publishers use a 15 ips reel-to-reel to play a master demo that they run their cassettes from.

There are many models on the market, and you can get ones that have almost any imaginable function. I find that the high-speed features are well worth the extra dollars in terms of time saved. (You should realize, though, that you lose some of the signal when recording at a higher speed because the machines play back at half the speed you recorded at. But it still comes in handy when you need a tape copy in a hurry.) Don't skimp on your dubbing deck. You'll want your tapes to sound as good as your original demo. I have encountered too many demos that sound like they were dubbed over a phone in an electrical storm to neglect this point. If the deck no longer runs at the right speed either fix it or dump it. There's no reason not to make it right.

Also avoid common errors such as allowing the leader to cut off your song's intro, having another song previously recorded on the tape bleed through, or recording songs on the same tape at differing volumes. I know of a situation where someone reused a tape that had had three songs on it. The producer recorded the second song that the writer didn't even know he had pitched! It was a rather embarrassing situation. By using a blank single-song cassette, you can avoid this problem. It only takes a few extra minutes to do it right.

CHECK EVERY PITCH

I don't care how good your equipment is—always double-check every pitch that goes out with your name on it. Wires come loose, the wrong buttons get pushed, and sometimes tapes don't come out just the way you'd like. I've had top-of-the-line high chrome cassettes sound like they went through the dishwasher when I played them back, and no one can explain why. Blame it on lunar phases or sun spots; there isn't any rational explanation why things sometimes go wrong. So I repeat: Check every pitch. Every songwriter I've ever talked to about this (and I've done it myself) has handed a blank cassette to someone who agreed to set aside precious time to listen.

When I know that I'm going to be sitting down with a producer or artist I will make up a special tape of three or four songs chosen specifically for them. I leave this tape with them if they like any of my material. I also bring along a few master cassettes with five songs per side if they ask for something else or want to spend all afternoon listening. I don't bring every song I've written every time out.

If you've done your research and chosen the proper songs you should have no problem getting past this stage and into the actual producer's stack of songs to listen to. When you submit your songs directly to a record label or manager your song will, hopefully, be passed on directly to the artist himself after an initial screening process. Someone from the label or the producer's office will usually call and ask you to put the song on hold (more on this in Chapter Eight).

When a song is on hold they will normally inform you that the artist is planning to go into the studio in *x* number of days or months and will be taking your song in with them. Asking to put a song on hold does not obligate the artist to use it. This is not a contract and there are no guarantees. But the closer to the actual recording date your songs are placed on hold, the better you can feel. I like getting songs to an artist just before he or she goes into the studio or in the middle of the actual recording process. Just like us, artists may have a few "old favorite" songs that they've dreamed of recording but like most songwriters they tend to favor their latest discovery or creation.

COST-EFFECTIVE DEMOS

You want your demos to sound great, thinking your songs will have a better chance of being picked up, but be careful. The recording studio is the easiest place to waste time and money. The tiniest error in choosing the wrong musician or vocalist costs you every single minute you're not getting what you want. Don't compromise. Work with professionals and either take control of the session yourself or hire someone to come in and produce for you. Too many times every musician in the room thinks that he's the producer and they all want to tell you how the song should go. This can usually be avoided by letting the musician you can communicate with most readily be the leader. If you're still faced with someone else trying

31

to tell you what you should or shouldn't do, put your foot down. It's your song and the musicians are working for you. All too often, especially when you're first starting out, it's easy to choose the wrong player on someone else's recommendation.

Always pay attention to the engineer and demand that he pay attention to your wishes as well. I've worked in studios where the phone rang continually and songs that should have taken an hour or two to record wound up taking all day. Recording is a concentrated effort and demands 100 percent attention of all the parties involved. If there's an overdub going on, don't let the other musicians stage a reunion in the control room. It's not that hard to retain control and still have fun. You already know in your head how you want the song to sound. It doesn't cost any more to hire professional musicians than to use your friends who will probably take much longer due to lack of experience. Hopefully they won't feel slighted and will understand your need to spend every penny wisely.

If you decide to use friends anyway, be sure to rehearse the songs at home before you go into the studio so you can find out how long it's going to take to learn a tricky introduction, or if the lead player is professional-sounding enough. Use this time to choose the right key for each song. When demoing more than one song at a time (the cost-effective way), try not to record similar songs in the same key back to back. Such repetition is boring, and there's nothing worse than musicians who sound bored. You want the demo to put even more magic into the song. Often, a great singer and a good keyboard player will be all you need. You can put down a number of songs with a simple arrangement and then listen back to see if they warrant more production. Don't make records. That's the producer's job, and he has thousands to spend where you have hundreds. Don't fake instruments. If you don't have a banjo, don't have the guitar player make his guitar sound like a banjo. It will only cheapen the overall effect of your demo. Too many times people get carried away with sound effects, fake strings, flutes, and whatever. Personally, I find most of these additions distracting to the lyric. A good song doesn't require these efforts. It's much too easy to bury a song under over-production. If you don't believe me, turn on the radio.

The studio will provide you with a final mix that will be on a reel-to-reel. Reel-to-reel tape recorders are very expensive and if you don't already have one, you can ask the studio to make you a master cassette on a high-quality tape to dub copies from. Just make sure to keep your deck as clean as possible.

FRESH TAPES ARE AN ABSOLUTE MUST. Cassettes are cheap enough that you don't need to be recording your demos over some old already-recorded tape. If you want to reuse tapes that have been returned to you then go out and buy a bulk eraser. This device will remove the entire prerecorded signal. When you use the erase head on your tape deck it will usually be in the same alignment as whatever was recorded with the same machine but someone else's deck can sometimes pick up a ghost of the previous signal. The tape will sound perfectly fine at home but may sound unintelligible on another machine due to bleed-through. It's much easier just to use fresh tape. This may seem obvious to most readers but I've heard too many tapes with this problem not to mention it.

A surprisingly large number of beginning publishers and writers will go down to the local stereo shop or drugstore and purchase very expensive ninety-minute cassettes to pitch one or two songs on. This isn't necessary. Get out the phone book and find yourself a wholesaler of cassettes who has six- and twelve-minute cassettes made from the same tape stock as the nineties you were using. The savings will be well worth the effort. Check every cassette you make to make sure that the entire song or songs were recorded. Machines make errors. If you insist on reusing someone else's tape make sure that it's blank all the way through.

I know of a situation where a tape copier at a publisher's grabbed up a tape that had come in through the mail and put the one song he wanted to pitch on side A. He checked the tape, heard his song, and sent it off. The producers called back a week later to say that they were crazy about the *second* song on the tape.

The publisher realized there must have been a song left on the tape. There was a frantic search, luckily someone recognized the singer, and they were able to track down the lucky songwriter and publisher who had stumbled into a cut. It's very easy to see how this situation developed. Most songs are generally between two-and-a-half and three-and-a-half minutes long. The song from the penny-pinching publisher, who hadn't bothered to erase the rest of the tape, made it appear that both songs were coming from the same source. Don't let this happen to you.

KEEPING YOUR BUSINESS GOING

Many factors enter into the decision on whether or not to invest in a home studio. You'll have to evaluate your own situation, investigate your options, and decide what's best for you. I have resisted getting too deeply involved in a home studio, which would be a money-saving option for any self-publisher, because I can accomplish more by letting someone else be the engineer and equipment repair person. Without those hassles, I have more time to write and pitch my songs. It would be fun to have my own studio to play in but I would probably never leave the house! I like to finish what I start and a home studio is an unfinished project if ever there was one. There's always one more part to upgrade and one more take on the guitar solo. I try to be time-conscious. The quality has to be at a certain level but I do keep reminding myself, "It's only a demo."

As an independent songwriter/publisher, give yourself a weekly schedule to make x number of pitches or finish x number of songs. Find time to work in the early morning and drop off your pitches at the post office on your way to work or your first appointment. Pitching songs can be done by mail from anywhere there's a mailbox. I know songwriters who work in remote teepees without electricity and songwriters who have honed their craft by ancient lakes in central Mexico where the current needed to run their tape recorder was as mercurial as the weather. You can't make excuses like "If I were only in L.A." or "Nashville's just too far away." The mail comes and goes six days a week. Send that tape tomorrow. Procrastination is a creative person's worst enemy.

When I first started giving songwriting seminars I would often ask participants for tapes of songs that I liked. By the time the small percentage who actually sent me a tape got around to it I had usually forgotten what project I wanted a tape for. If you had asked me for a tape when I was starting out you can be sure that that tape would have beaten you home.

There is no surefire way to predict how successful any one recording might be. Sure, there are the Michael Jacksons, the Alabamas, and the rest of the big pop acts that can make you financially stable from just one single but these are also the hardest acts to get material to. But no doubt there was also a time in all of these stars' respective careers when almost anyone could have walked in with material that was better than they were getting. In pop music you will run into more self-contained songwriter/performers, but a good lyricist or melody person can probably find a place for their work if they do the proper research. Which brings us to the next chapter.

Doing your homework

If I thought that I could predict what style of song the public would rush out and buy tomorrow I would not be trying to make my living as a songwriter. I would get an office right in the middle of the record labels and offer my services for a fee to anyone who'd believe me. There are record producers and chart watchers who do just this type of fortune-telling for a living, but it's way too "guessy" a game for most of us. Rather than predict the future, let's look at certain trends that seem to come back again and again.

Every decade or so music seems to return to its "roots" and one hears more acoustic-oriented music, be it the folkies' of the sixties or today's "new age" musicians' or just today's rock act twanging away at a steel-string guitar. The listening public, like anyone else, needs a break, and the music industry quiets down for a bit. There's always room for a big-voiced Elvis type and there's always room for an all-girl group whether it's rock and roll or country. There are always certain voids to be filled and you need to take these into con- -sideration when you're pitching your songs.

FILLING A VOID

As noted earlier, I personally tend to write a lot of novelty songs. Publishers have always told me that novelty songs are hard to pitch. I disagree. If you go through any book of the top ten pop records of the last fifteen years you'll be amazed to see how many novelty songs have made it to the top. The acts that had novelty hits were usually complete unknowns beforehand and many never repeated their success, but some songwriter or publisher got lucky, if only for a little while.

The public likes to laugh. They also like a good instrumental every now and then even though most publishers will tell you that instrumentals are dead. Look for the holes that aren't being filled by everybody else out there. Be a trend-setter yourself. Familiarizing yourself with types of music other than the music you're trying to write can give you a definite edge when you're asked to come up with something "new." Tunnel vision is rampant in the music industry and everyone loves to hear something truly original.

An even more disturbing trend keeps surfacing in the country music field, where certain rock and roll songwriters think they can turn a fast buck by cranking out country tunes. These writers have no regard for their country audience (if anything, they regard them as semiliterate). Their home and car radios are tuned to the local heavy metal station; they only tune in to the country station in hopes of hearing one of their own songs. These writers aren't writing songs; they're writing parodies.

If you're going to be successful you need to try and improve the type of music you truly admire, creating something new rather than parodies. Don't try to make a rock and roll band country by adding a steel guitar. It's embarrassing to listen to. It's bad rock and roll and even worse country music. By creating the best possible song one can avoid all of the above pitfalls. Good songs will fit many styles; the singer or instrumental backing will be the deciding factor.

KNOW YOUR AUDIENCE

Don't pander or write down to your audience. Choose acts that you'd be proud to have record your songs and try to create material that will be as good as or better than what they've already done. It looks very simple in writing. But it takes a lot of research and sometimes sheer luck to do this consistently enough to make a living at it. It *can* be done, and your odds for success will be greatly increased with the amount of research you do. Knowing your audience will pay off. An author once observed that he was glad that songwriters like Paul Simon weren't trying to write like they were fifteen-year-olds with their first guitars. Simon's successful lyrical attitude is more one of "back before you were born . . ." People appreciate honesty and integrity in songs.

Are you trying to write songs for your own peer group or are you attempting to reach a specialized group of people? You need to be able to focus in on record buyers the same way you would focus a camera.

Let's take Johnny Cash's fans for an example. It's a gross general-ization to believe that all of his fans drive pick-up trucks and have too many relatives in Arkansas. Don't help perpetrate these stereo-types. If you're writing down to your audience you're heading in the wrong direction before you even get your pen on paper.

It's perfectly all right to use humor in your music, especially with an artist like Cash who, though rugged and dramatic, has had novelty songs become some of his biggest hits. The difference was that the novelty songs he had success with weren't attacking his au-dience. They were describing characters the audience knew.

Avoid stereotypes. The days of the country song heroine, for ex-ample, who's "so dumb she doesn't know I'm cheating and drink-ing" are over. You can't fool your audience. Whether country fans or heavy metal fans, they're very "tuned in"—and they can spot a paro-dy a mile away.

I don't mind heavy metal music, but for me to try to write it would be ridiculous. I don't understand the language. It's important to write what you know. Even the songs created for Broadway shows and movie themes have little in common with the songs that are hits on the radio. True, they borrow from today's hits, but lyrical-ly they are too much a part of a production to stand alone.

The rise of MTV and other video networks has also created a false demand for songs that are merely background music for vid-eos. These songs would not work without the accompanying video stimuli and they will be forgotten in a matter of months. I like to write songs that can stand on their own with just voice and one in-strument. If I have to show you two people and a Hollywood movie set to get my message across, I'm not doing my job.

It's important to first understand the style of music you're try-ing to write and then try to improve on what's already been done. I have mentioned it elsewhere but I am constantly running into song-writers and publishers who are writing down to their audience. It's easy to see why they don't get many songs recorded.

LEARNING HOW TO SPOT TRADEMARK STYLES

The artist or producer you've selected to pitch your songs to will want to believe that the songs you've sent were chosen after careful thought and research. I can remember watching Lacy J. Dalton going through bags of tapes and remarking again and again, "Why are these people sending me these songs?" The songs would invariably be either very fifties country girl-singer material or else very clever and cute play-on-words songs. None of them were remotely like anything she had recorded previously. There were certain publishers who were notorious for never even coming close to anything she might be interested in. A quick listen to any of Lacy's singles or albums will reveal that she likes blues-oriented rock and roll with a few minor chords and extremely well-crafted country story-songs about realistic situations.

Spend as much time as you can listening to the artists you've selected as most likely to do your material. Try and choose three of your own songs for that artist and then try to think of other songs you may have heard on other albums that this artist could do. Is the music compatible? Does the vocal phrasing match? The easiest style point to spot is the way an artist will phrase a song. Some artists can sing a lot of words and not sound like he or she is racing through a song, and some artists need songs with a lot of breaths between the words and very simple lyrics.

Great singers who would even sound good singing the phone book often record songs not for the songs' lyrical content but because of their own vocal range and the fact that they and their producer know that the way their voice will break on a certain note will "sell" the song. Often, when your friends tell you that a song would be perfect for a certain artist it is this part of an artist's style that they recognize in your song.

I purposely try to match my demo singers with the artist I am pitching to but I don't want them to try and sound exactly like that specific artist. The point is to find someone who sounds as if he or she enjoys singing your song and to write song lyrics that your intended singer can identify with. A lot of pitches get passed over without being listened to at all because the singer or producer or whoever is screening songs knows that the act they're looking for isn't interested in a song about someone else's mother, or whatever the title may be.

Go back and look at the selected artist's last few albums and see what kind of ideas you get from just reading the titles of the songs without listening to the lyrics and music. If every other song has "cheatin' " and "drinking" in the title you can feel safe pitching your latest cheatin' and drinking song. But a lot of performers have never recorded any songs about cheating and drinking and don't bother listening to songs with those words in the title when looking for new material. This by no means should lead you to believe that your titles need to be generic, but they must be something the artist has an interest in. Be on the artist's wave length. Be fresh and original. Let him know that you've done your homework.

Research groups as thoroughly as individual artists. There are guitar-oriented groups and groups that want three-part harmonies throughout their songs and groups that will have one or two cuts by each member on an album, so you really have to be a psychiatrist to figure out who you're pitching to. It's like learning a foreign language. Take it a phrase at a time. I listen to an album over and over again, trying to find a thread that ties the ten cuts together. Even after all that, you'll find some artists are tough to categorize and may even appear directionless. They're as at home singing blues as they are a sappy ballad. You have to figure that these artists are trying to give the public what it wants and it then becomes a matter of researching the public's tastes. It's all too easy to become isolated in one style of music and lose touch with what is selling in another. Learn to listen.

HOW TO READ A RECORD ALBUM

The importance of research is all too often ignored by publishers and songwriters alike. But it's a case of INPUT = OUTPUT. The more you learn about the music industry the less frustrating it will be. For the beginning songwriter, constant research is a strong ally. If the lead singer of a band you're pitching songs to just got married he's probably not recording a lot of material about how the "fire just died at home."

You need to carefully research each artist you want to pitch to. The first step is to establish how they sound. Go down to your nearest chain record store. Ask the clerk if they have any current albums or singles by the act. Purchase these records or—if the clerk is so obliged—ask him to please play one of the cuts for you. Let's say that you've decided to go all out and have purchased the latest LP by the artist you want to pitch to. You now have a key to many different approaches to the artist.

40

Let's say you've purchased the new John Smith LP. All you see on the record jacket is an airbrushed photo of some guy with good teeth and an even better haircut looking very contented. No blues for this guy, unless he's spoofing his audience. Pull the record out. The writer-publisher information should be written under the title of each of the ten selections. I put the record on my stereo without reading who wrote what. Then I make a cup of coffee and get out a scratch pad. Start with the first song on side A. This is usually the strongest cut on the album and the only one that radio program directors will give a listen to if they're not already familiar with Smith. Write down the title and a brief note or two on the style. It should read something like, "Baby's in Love—power chords, Cecil B. De-Mille chorus. Great hook." Go on to the next cut.

Producers rarely stack up the favored cuts one, two, three, side A, but it does happen sometimes so be prepared. Usually the second cut will be one of the artist's favorites and a complete tempo change from the first and third songs. The third song is often the first single. (They're saving the first cut for a one-two punch.) It may have many of the same production elements as cut one and may feature the same solo instruments. You notice the mix is funny and you wonder if the album wasn't produced by the drummer. No one ever seems to hear enough of his own instrument. Make a note to check whether the producer is a drummer. The fourth cut doesn't fit any category. The song has got to be at least five minutes long and is very different from anything else so far. The last cut sounds a lot like the first and third cuts. Make a note of its feel and turn the record over. Repeat the process on side two. Pay careful attention to the last cut on side two, as this is often a single position. I have always assumed that they did this as a service to disk jockeys who don't have time to fumble around cueing up a cut.

I usually don't even read the liner notes or album sleeve until I've listened to the entire album. Then I read that the drummer was a coproducer—which explains his prominence in the mix. (It's something to keep in mind when mixing demos especially for that artist in the future.) The other producer is a well-known one who's never shown any publishing affiliations.

Producers who are affiliated with a publishing company are an everyday problem for independent publishers and anyone else trying to get songs to certain artists. Here's why.

41

Once upon a time a young aspiring producer needed an office and a secretary. He had been a studio musician and had come to know many of the publishers through demos he had played on for them. One of the demo singers had attracted the attention of the head of the record label, who asked the aspiring young producer to get some of the guys together and produce some sides. The would-be producer went around to his weekly demo sessions and got some really good songs from the various songwriters who'd supported him for years. They gladly gave him permission to cut their songs on his newly discovered act. The act charted and he was on his way to the top. One of the publishers had a brand new office building, and "gave" the producer an office with all the things a young producer would need: a phone and a desk and a secretary to take his calls. When the young producer needed songs he only had to open his door and all of the staff writers would stream in. The kind publisher got lots and lots of his songs recorded and after a while songwriters who didn't work for the host publisher couldn't even get the aspiring young producer on the phone.

These albums are very easy to spot. All the songs not written by the artist—and often as not those, too—are published by one parent company. This will be the case on any artist's album these producers work with. It's a lot harder to get on one of these albums without giving up your publishing. If they still want your song without taking their cut you can bet that it's not just for an album cut.

Luckily, this John Smith album looked very hopeful. Only two songs had been published by the same company and the artist was a co-writer on both. The rest of the material had come from a variety of sources. Major publishers accounted for three of the songs, including the first single, but none of those writers were household names. The rest of the songs seemed to have come from lesser-known independent companies like yours or mine. It's always a pleasure to know that artists and producers are also doing some research in finding new material. Too often today's material is a rehash of oldies covers and barely disguised rip-offs of the latest trends. Here was an artist with good teeth, good hair, *and* integrity.

BUILDING YOUR OWN RESEARCH LIBRARY
There are, unfortunately, few research libraries available to the beginning songwriter, so you must build your own. It always amazes

me to go to songwriters' homes to collaborate and discover that un-less they're hiding the books in the attic they don't ever take the time to read. If there is a bookshelf it is often as not filled with text-books or required reading from their days in college. There might be a few music magazines like *Rolling Stone* lying around but their source of inspiration for new songs is obviously not from the print-ed word. I can't stress how important a strong sense of good story-telling is when you're trying to get your song recorded. If your lyric and music are matched and the story in your song excites the listen-er your odds for getting that material recorded are much higher than someone with "just another love song." It doesn't matter what type of music you are writing: the better the lyric, the better the song.

There have been hundreds of books written about every aspect of the music business. Everyone from producers to promoters to Elvis's second cousin has put his or her personal story down on pa-per. You could spend hundreds of dollars a month and not keep up with the constant flow. In addition to this wealth of new material, music foundations and university presses are reprinting older titles. It's easier every day to accumulate information about the workings of the music industry.

If I'm asked for material for an established artist I will research that person like the Mission Impossible team would research some South American dictator. I'm sure you remember the opening se-quences where they handed out the clues. Learn to treat each act that you feel could record your songs in the same way.

Find interviews with the act. More than once I've remembered an artist talking about who their influences were, be it the Beatles or Sam Cooke or Hank Williams, Sr. After listening to the artist's re-cording, I then went back and listened to the influence's recordings and used what I picked up from both to help select the songs I would pitch.

Some of you may not even be sure what artist you want to pitch your songs to. Your first step should be to establish a current artist roster for each of the record labels that you might approach. It doesn't matter what kind of material you're publishing and pitch-ing—it's the same basic process for every style. *Billboard* and *Cash-box* will have special issues devoted to the styles of music you're most interested in, and there will probably be page after page of ads promoting the acts signed to each label. Get out a file folder and set up a separate file for each label with the act, the producer, and the contact person. By this you should try to establish who is responsible for screening new material. Is it someone in the artist and repertoire department at the label? Is there more than one producer? All of this information needs to be gathered on every act that you will be pitching songs to. As acts change producers and jump labels, you will scratch them off one list and add them to another.

Read the business news sections in the trade magazines and take a close look at the photos that show so-and-so just signing with a new company or producer. You will have to check the charts to find out who the current producers are or else make a trip down to the local record store to see who's working with who. After you've got your basic lists it's relatively easy to eliminate the acts that probably wouldn't do your songs and concentrate on the acts you feel you're creating great material for. These should prove to be constantly changing lists, with a new name always being added or someone being dropped. Update constantly. These files will be a good source for information when you do get a record out and want to know immediately who else the label will be putting support behind. Rather than going through the charts trying to spot all of the acts on XYZ records and their subsidiaries, you can pull out your file and know exactly who the competition for promotion will be from within the label.

Along with these files you can also keep a separate listing (such as a Rolodex card) for each act with producer, manager, and other contacts listed. You should also keep track of the songs that you've pitched to each artist and producer. I've seen some publishers who've set up computer programs that even have a space for the producer's comments on the songs. When a producer or his representative tells you, "I really think that's a great song but we've already got too many ballads" or "I wish I'd had that song when I was doing Jane Doe's last album," take notes. There are too many labels and too many artists for you to remember what everyone said. It's humanly impossible to remember all the information that you can use to get your songs recorded. The more organized a system you have, the easier it will be to track your progress. The last thing you want is to be asked for material by an artist or producer and not know what you've pitched them before.

You need to learn to think like a record label, always on the lookout for a new outlet for your material. If someone on a competitive label is selling a certain type of record, expect a clone on another label. Often as not the clone may be more receptive to your material.

In the past year I have had some success pitching songs to a new female artist who just released her first album on a major label. Everyone agrees that she's a strong contender to be the "next big thing." How did I know? I was visiting a fellow songwriter who had just had a song recorded by this artist on a small folk label. I listened to her album and enjoyed the songs and her singing. She'd already recorded one of my friend's songs so I assumed that she was open to outside material even though she wrote most of her own songs. Too many songwriters are intimidated by the fact that the artist writes his or her own material and tend not to pitch songs to these acts. If I were a commercial recording artist and someone pitched me a song that I wished I'd written that fit my style of singing I'd be happy to popularize it. (Let's not forget that most of the listening public thinks that the singer must have also written the song anyway.)

The importance of research cannot be overemphasized. There are books that will tell you what chart records each act from, say, 1967 to 1986 has had in almost every style of music and you can then get the artist's older albums and listen to what their most successful records were. Eliminate the guesswork. Be methodical and your research will become a habit that you don't even notice. Your local public library won't have every new book on the music business but they will have *Billboard* and other music publications to go through. Once you get started and have chosen a few select acts that are most likely to accept your material it will be easy to expand your research library.

THE SONGWRITER'S BOOKSHELF

Anyone trying to be a professional songwriter outside of one of the major music centers will have to develop their own system to stay in touch with what's happening in the segment of the industry in which they're trying to get their songs recorded. I find it amazing that very few songwriters have an interest in the history of their craft beyond speculating how much money some famous writer like Johnny Mercer or Harold Arlen must have made. The more you know about the industry the easier it will be to plan your next move. I'll start with a few books that I consider essential and then move along to the various trade publications and magazines.

Songwriter's Market is an annual directory published by Writer's Digest Books. You may have already purchased this year's *Songwriter's Market*. Many writers have the vague impression that the directory is for absolute beginners who have no idea where to start and that it is a hotbed of fly-by-night song sharks, etc. Not so! The *Songwriter's Market* is worth having and keeping around if only for the industry profiles or the lists of sheet music publishers and record companies. The editors are doing our work for us, going over *Billboard* and other trade publications looking for each new entry. Another factor to consider is that all entries are screened as best as possible to keep out the crooks. It's a very good tool that is much too often overlooked.

If your specialty is country music, there are many books on that subject but one of the best on songs is *Sing Your Heart Out Country Boy* by Dorothy Horstman, published by the Country Music Foundation. In 1977 Dorothy Horstman interviewed the writers of over three hundred classic country songs. The correct lyric to each song is printed along with a couple of paragraphs by the writer on how they happened to write their best song. This is a very humbling but informative book and is indispensable for anyone wanting to write country music. It was long out of print, but the Country Music Foundation at the Hall of Fame has gotten Horstman to update the book with many newer songs and promises to keep it available. Some other books worth seeking out are *Lyrics on Several Occasions* by Ira Gershwin, *Happy with the Blues: Harold Arlen* by Edward Jablowski, *The Street Where You Live* by Alan J. Lerner, and *Writings and Drawings* by Bob Dylan. All of the above books are an excellent place to start building your own inspiration bank. There are also books available on Hoagy Carmichael, Johnny Mercer, Hank Williams, and many of the other great songwriters. Most of the better-known rock and rhythm-and-blues performers have had biographies written. Publishers figure that an artist who has sold hundreds of thousands of records ought to sell a few thousand books.

A problem here is that this type of book tends to go out of print very quickly and bookstores aren't known to stock a very wide selection of songwriter biographies. The best place to look is in used bookstores and second-hand shops. The same holds true for your standard "show business personality" books. There are hundreds of these flooding the market, some of them very well written. Many of the ones on pop performers tend to be a little lightweight but the books on Tin Pan Alley and the older singers usually have some valuable insights into song plugging in the thirties and forties. Sometimes you'll have to read an entire biography to find that one paragraph that will help you get a song recorded sometime in the future.

Every time I go to a new bookstore I make a point to check the music book section and browse through a few of the new arrivals. It's heartening to see that many of the older classics like *Lyrics on Several Occasions,* are now available again in paperback. The American public's perception of what a songwriter "does for a living" is grossly distorted from the reality. Buy books on songwriting and share them with your friends and family. It's the easiest way to learn your craft while earning your ticket to New York, Los Angeles, or Nashville. Too many writers arrive in those locales totally unprepared and spend valuable dollars and time learning basics they could have picked up at home. You might even be able to get your local public library to order some of these books for you and the next generations of songwriters.

Billboard is the number one weekly publication for the music industry. It is also very expensive to subscribe to, but you can usually find it in most public libraries and on the newsstands in any city. Besides the basic information such as the producer and publisher of a selected artist's latest hit, a songwriter can learn to predict when an artist is usually going to start looking for new material again by keeping a personal scorecard to help keep track of how many singles an artist has pulled from the album in current release. It's a rare exception for an artist to take more than three singles from any one record. About the time the third single is hitting the top twenty, the search for the next album's material intensifies.

Sometimes there will be only two singles but the public seems to demand at least three hits per album. If the artist hasn't changed producers and managers you should be getting your tape ready to pitch for the next record. I constantly talk to writers and publishers alike who figure I must have had some "inside" connection to tell me when to pitch to certain artists, but it's really no secret. It's simply research.

Another publication that can show you how well your songs are doing once they're recorded—and also give you extremely detailed charts—is *R&R,* or *Radio and Records.* Its pages list the top fifty songs in each category and give a lot of attention to developing records. You can actually watch a record break out across the country through *R&R*'s separate playlists from many cities. It's a very good newspaper format magazine, aimed at a more specialized reader than *Billboard.* As for *Rolling Stone, Spin, People,* etc., I read these magazines with a somewhat jaded eye. The amount of solid research-type information you're likely to get from these is limited. As general interest titles, these types of magazines seem to be more interested in creating trends rather than reporting on them. Every once in a while there'll be a great interview with some producer or artist but everyone knows what to expect from publications of this nature. The same holds true for the personality interviews found in men's magazines like *Playboy* and *Penthouse.* But that doesn't mean you should exclude such titles. I read everything I can get my hands on and will often pick up a very useful tidbit in a very obscure place. Leave no stone unturned.

Magazines like *Musician* are geared more towards career musicians and writers and a visit to a well-stocked newsstand will show that every style of music has its own specialized magazine like *Sing Out* for the folkies, and *Down Beat* for jazz lovers.

For anyone seriously interested in country song writing there's a monthly magazine called *Music Row* that carries great articles and some of the best reviews of all kinds of records by Nashville critics and writers. It's well worth the price of a subscription.

Every newsstand has magazines like *Song Hits, Country Song Hits,* and various others aimed at a specific audience. These are great to go through from time to time. They will usually have a lot of lyrics (helpful for checking out the competition) and some feature articles. You can also pick up magazines like *Frets* and *Guitar Player* to find out what's happening in the acoustic music field. Even more specialized magazines exist for jazz musicians, piano players, or almost any other discipline you can name. Learn as much as you can about the style of music you're trying to write. It will come in handy in the long run.

And you don't have to limit your magazine reading to the music field. There are also publications like *Writer's Digest* that, while not aimed at the songwriter, still are a source of inspiration through the long wait for that first hit and then whatever success follows.

TIP SHEETS

Many tip sheets are available for a monthly or yearly fee. These sheets try to stay on top of information like who's recording what kind of songs and how to get in touch with them. The tip sheets are best used to send songs to new acts one might not be that familiar with or to learn about changes in record labels and producers. I have personally never found these sheets to be that up to date and prefer to rely on the system I've already described to you—choosing the acts I feel would be most likely to record my songs and then paying attention to those acts on the *Billboard* charts.

I start sending songs out for consideration after the artist or group has released two singles from their current album. When the second single appears to be getting as high as it's going to go on the chart, I will send a single-song cassette to the artist in care of the producer and another to the manager or whoever I can track down who accepts material for the act. I don't expect to get my tape back. After a week or so I will call and see if someone has had an opportunity to listen to my song. Sometimes I'll be informed that the artist isn't planning to go back into the studio for a while so I make a note of when to try again. It doesn't take that much paperwork.

A much too common trend these days is what I call the "may the best man win syndrome." A label decides to let three or four different producers all try and find the best songs for an artist and then group these together in a hodge-podge of an album that doesn't have much cohesion. This is as confusing to those of us pitching songs as it must be to the artists themselves.

Unless the act has already established a strong sense of direction this would have to be a ridiculous way to go about making a record. I understand the concept, but albums need to be focused so that the listening public has an idea of what the artist is all about. The same holds true for the much too prevalent "so-and-so with friends" albums. The songs seem to be chosen more for the friends than for the artist, and it's often hard to figure what or even who to pitch to. I believe that your chances for getting a song recorded will be much greater if you can concentrate on one or two acts who appear to be willing to record outside material. The money you save on tip sheets can be better used building a reference library to go back to again and again.

THE PITCH

As an independent songwriter/publisher you should view yourself as the owner of a small boutique surrounded by towering warehouses full of goods similar to the ones you're selling, with one main difference: the amount of attention you can put into your pitches/ sales (see sidebar).

Your boutique/publishing company has to build a reputation for higher quality than the "warehouses" who may have greater variety. If you can get the quality of your material to a consistent level there is a place for you and your songs in the music business. Even if you have only one or two songs that you feel are at these levels you can start pitching and hoping that an artist will believe in the songs as much as you do.

PITCHING YOUR SONGS

Don't be scared to start small. As long as the performer will be doing a version of the song that you can be proud of, there's no reason not to let anyone use your material. Holding a song back waiting for some superstar to return your call is like sitting at home waiting for a record label to come ask you to record. It doesn't happen very often.

In 1985 Lewis Anderson was the BMI country writer of the year. A native of Louisiana, Lewis started playing guitar in bands in high school and fell into songwriting for these groups. When he moved to Los Angeles in the early seventies he already had a successful local group doing mostly original material.

Lewis wanted to keep part of his publishing and got into a co-publishing situation with some new contacts in L.A. The new contacts suggested that he might be interested in coproducing a solo act that was playing the clubs and working as an opening act for some better-known groups. One of the songs that Lewis gave the act

SELL YOUR SONGS, NOT YOUR PUBLISHING

I hesitate to ever use the word "sales" in connection with songwriting because I never recommend selling any part of the ownership of your song to ensure getting it recorded. Some producers or recording artists will agree to use your song only if you promise to sign over the publishing, or a part of the publishing, to them in return. Then it's theirs for the life of the copyright, and you really have to wonder if they're going to function as a publisher, re-demoing your song and pitching it to other acts. Letting others have a piece of your publishing leads to incredible confusion when you have some hits and want to get paid. They'll almost always want to administer the copyright as well, and you'll be waiting and wondering when or if they'll get around to accounting to you.

Getting a percentage of the publishing shouldn't influence whether someone records your song. The fear that someone else will record a good song and have a hit (without asking for the publishing) should be incentive enough. Don't waste time with a deal like this unless you can live with it for the life of the copyright.

I repeat: Don't give up your publishing to get your foot in the door. If you don't want to self-publish and you're looking for a publisher for your songs, or if another independent publisher is doing all of the legwork for you and deserves a fair percentage, that's another matter. There are companies in all the major music cities that will administer songs you get cut for a small percentage and they won't want to share ownership of the copyright (see "Administration Deals" in Chapter Six).

to record was heard by the Carpenters who used this act to open for them. They recorded Lewis's song and it appeared on an album that went gold. The Carpenters' guitar player in turn remembered how much he liked the song, and when he had an opportunity to produce Seals and Crofts, Lewis got his song on one of their better-selling albums. Similar situations also got Lewis's copublished songs on gold and platinum albums by Kenny Rogers, Crystal Gayle, and Helen Reddy.

The music business is a maze and very few of us are anywhere near the inner circle, so we need to find clever paths that will at least put us close to the act we hope will eventually record our songs. Lewis Anderson had no premeditated plan to get a Seals and

Crofts cut. It just worked out that way because 1) The song was there and 2) The right parties were exposed to the song. The Carpenters and their band heard the opening act do the song night after night. Most importantly, Lewis had given the song to a relatively unknown performer. If he had said, "You can't have this—I'm holding it back for Seals and Crofts," he might still be waiting. When he first wrote the song he had no way of knowing the path it would travel. Every songwriter hopes to get this kind of mileage out of every song he writes but only a select few songs will ever see the light of day.

BELIEVING IN YOUR MATERIAL

I was in a small music store recently when I was introduced to one of the employees who told me that he enjoyed my material. He said he had once been a songwriter himself but "Mr. Blank up in Nashville" had gotten his best songs and then nothing had happened so he'd given up on writing and gone back to playing and teaching guitar. I didn't really know what to say. I agreed with him that publishers will often be very excited about a song and then when nothing happens immediately will put it on a shelf where many a great song rests, never to be heard again. But I had a hard time grasping the concept that Mr. Blank had gotten his best songs. My best song will, hopefully, be the one that I write tomorrow. Over the years I've left some very well written songs with some very unappreciative publishers but they haven't gotten my "best" song and I hope they never will.

You've got to approach each new song idea as an improvement on what you have previously written. Songwriting, like any other skill, improves with practice. Years ago I studied art and developed a pretty good sense of eye to hand control. I could look at an apple and draw a picture of it without wearing out an eraser. I'm sure if I tried an even simpler artistic exercise right now I'd be embarrassed by the results. You have to stay in practice.

I wrote hundreds of country songs before I realized that I had been writing Hollywood versions of what a country story should be. The concept of the songs—e.g., drinking, you broke my heart—may have been classifiable as country music but they were parodies and didn't come from the heart. Again, it's the songs that have a fresh approach and come from the heart that you can get recorded

53

no matter what the odds are. Self-doubt will be there at every turn but you can't let early frustrations slow you down. Study the style of music you want to create and immerse yourself in it. You need to be ready to get in over your head, to take some chances. All they can say is no. Press on—there's always another act coming into the public's view.

PITCHING TO LABEL A&R REPS

Each record label will have an artist and repertoire (A&R) person, someone who's supposed to be constantly finding new material for that label's artists. They screen all the material received at the front desk and through the mailroom. Unfortunately many of the major labels have recently started refusing to accept tapes that aren't from "major publishers we deal with on a regular basis." This is a sad development but you shouldn't be discouraged by this turn of events. "Goin' Gone" wasn't published by this breed of publisher and enough successful records by writers like us should hopefully open the doors again.

Only the major labels refuse to listen to unsolicited tapes, and if you really want to get through to them the right letter of inquiry will probably go a long way. I've had songs sent at the specific request of the head A&R person sent back with a form letter because some intern working for college credit didn't bother to read my cover letter. The song was later cut by another artist on another label.

Here's how it works in an ideal situation. Songs pitched to a certain artist—say, Randy Travis—will be set aside and sent to his representative whenever the pile gets too big. When the label knows for certain that Travis is going into the studio in a couple of weeks they will intensify their search for songs for him. It's helpful to keep in mind that most labels have a roster of at least twenty artists who all need two albums' worth of material a year. The A&R person would have to be a musical fanatic to keep track of the styles and musical directions of twenty different people. And, often as not, there will be a couple of artists that she can't stand.

If your songs are not selected for a recording project, just remember that it could be for one of any number of reasons. Songs get lost in the shuffle very easily. I have found a lot of A&R people rely much too heavily on one or two major publishers who can always come up with "something" rather than actively search out new material. We all have a favorite restaurant that can usually serve at least one dish that we like. The major publishers can usually come up with at least a couple of acceptable songs, and the labels will do their best to keep them at the top of the list when they're looking for material. Once again, you have to have material that is at the same level as a "major" and hopefully a bit more original. I've placed songs with one member of an A&R department one week and then called the next week to be told that absolutely no one was cutting at a label with a roster as long as my arm. It's hard to know when to wave the white flag.

WHAT HAPPENS AFTER THE PITCH

The major labels can be very slow in responding to unsolicited tapes, so be as professional as possible. Don't put a tape in the mail on a Monday and expect them to have listened to it by Thursday morning. Your tape will probably be in the pile to go through after the tapes from better-known writers and publishers are screened. If your title is intriguing enough you may get listened to a little sooner. Don't give up just because no one calls to thank you for your submission. You just have to hope for the best and leave no path untried if you really think you've got the right songs for a certain artist. I was talking to a songwriter/publisher who has been incredibly successful. He compared pitching songs to shooting a shotgun in a forest. You swear that you were aiming right for the heart of the tree but when you get up close to look for a hole there's no sign that you were anywhere near the target.

Your only consolation is that artist and repertoire people are also changing labels and careers at almost as fast a rate as artists do and a good song is going to be a good song forever. They may not like any of your new songs but don't let it stop your work. Every now and then you'll get a call saying that they actually opened one of your tapes and are passing it on to the artist or artist's producer. There are some extremely qualified A&R people in the industry who have revolutionized their label's image by their aggressive approach to finding new talent and equally fresh material. Labels with dead rosters have been rejuvenated overnight and regional types of music sweep the country like a tidal wave. If one person rejects your song, submit it to someone else who may be more likely to give unknown talent a chance.

SELF-CONTAINED ACTS

The singer/songwriters of the seventies have been replaced by a whole new group of singer/songwriters who can also produce their own records. Like many other artists they find themselves looking for outside material when the time and toil of being on the road takes away their own writing time. There will also be situations where an intelligent songwriter/artist will seek out the kind of songs that he's never been able to write himself. I've had good luck pitching up-tempo songs to artists who up until then were best known for ballads. The A&R department may not be privy to the fact that the artist wants radically different material so your pitches should be very carefully tailored for the artist in this situation. The label rep has to be able to hear your song and hear their artist singing it without too much strain on the imagination.

If the act is keyboard oriented, don't send a voice-guitar demo. Every day new acts are added to a roster somewhere and old acts try to continue with whatever success they've already had. The search for new material never stops.

PITCHING TO MANAGERS, AGENTS, AND ATTORNEYS

Pitching to an artist's record company is not the only way to get a tape to that artist. There are many other contacts close to the artist, and going to one of these people may be a more direct route. They're often more accessible than the artist or producer or the A&R person with a dozen acts to deal with.

MANAGERS

It is relatively easy to find out who an artist's manager is and pitch songs to him. The manager is usually thanked on the back of the record album. The record sleeve may not tell you who wrote the songs or played the instruments, but it will almost always state: "Manager . . . for Booking Information . . .", etc. The *Billboard Talent and Touring Directory* lists hundreds of artists' managers, but since managers come and go rather quickly with some artists, a phone call or query letter can get you the latest information.

Managers want hit singles. The artist and the producer want hit singles too, but they also have their artistic sides to gratify so they may cut a song that radio would never play. The manager knows that hits mean better shows and that means better money. When it's been announced that the artist is about to record, the manager will usually receive almost as many tapes as the producer or the record label. Every manager that I've known has listened to almost every tape sent to his artist. A good manager does more than wake up hoping for that one song that can become a career anthem. He dreams of TV spectaculars and months in Vegas and an endless percentage off the top. He likes to believe that he knows how the artist should sound even more so than the artist himself. That's a manager's job. Once again, you should be as professional as possible in all your pitches but especially so here. Only pitch your best song. The manager hasn't the time or inclination to give any writer an hour to go through ten "hits" unless he's specifically called and said, "Please send us anything you've got." This will sometimes happen when the songs and the artist seem to be extremely compatible but it's a rare situation.

The good point is that he will listen with hopeful ears and is less likely to give a damn about who's got the publishing during the initial screening for acceptable material. Most management companies are also publishers, so be prepared to be approached if their artist decides to record one of your songs. (See "Copublishing," Chapter Six.) If you have a smash for their artist they'll lobby for it like it was one of their own songs, especially if the act is just starting out or on the comeback trail. Successful managers sometimes call songwriters whose work they like and ask them to create material for their artists. They will also attend writers' nights and listen for songs on other artists' albums, always listening for that special something that will catapult their act to the top. Every manager would love to have a self-contained act like the Beatles, but even they chose to record outside songs from time to time. If you really feel that you've got the right material, contact the act's manager.

AGENTS AND CLUB OWNERS
Agents are another viable path to the recording artist, and some booking agencies actively seek material for their touring acts. They're looking for hits, just like managers, but agents will generally

just pass material on to artists through the road manager or by mail. Your tape can often arrive a day late, and every artist I've ever visited at home seemed to have shopping bags full of unlistened-to cassettes in every closet. Again, there are exceptions to the rules.

Club owners will also have contact with acts that are appearing in their clubs, and if you regularly attend shows, you should let them know that you are a local songwriter. Work with the local band. The band will be opening shows for the acts you're trying to reach, and more than one songwriter that I know has gotten a song cut when the headliner sat down and listened to the opening act.

It's a case of starting out at a level where you are with your peers. You can't walk up to a superstar's bus with a cassette in hand and expect to be let on board, but you do stand a chance of having one of the band members from the opening act tell one of the headliner's band members about the great local songwriter—you. You can probably become quite popular with the local band if you pay them to do your demo and then allow them to perform your songs.

ATTORNEYS AND YOU

In Nashville there are—surprisingly—only a dozen or so full-time music lawyers. There are plenty of firms that list "entertainment law" as one of their services, but the *right* music lawyer can be an incredibly strong ally in your attempts at getting your songs heard. Some firms get so many tapes that they have a full-time A&R person who screens the tapes of hopefuls seeking record deals.

Lawyers who specialize in music law should know as much about the music business as they do copyright law. They are the ones who draw up the agreements for those lucky individuals who are at a money-making level. They know who's who and can often predict a new label's lifespan much more accurately than the investors.

Most states do not certify specialists in any area of the law, so you have to do your research and find out who's recommended by those you trust. Most lawyers aren't publishers but they will have clients who are. They also are in regular contact with artists, and in the process of working with you may pass your material on to another client. But don't think that you can call the various music law firms and ask for a client roster. It doesn't work that way. If they hear your songs and believe that they are good enough to pass along, they usually will. Deals of every kind are made everyday. A good lawyer will improve your image in any business dealing. Don't kid yourself into thinking you can read a contract all by yourself. There are well-known producers and artists who have lost literally hundreds of thousands of dollars because they didn't have a lawyer review their contracts for them. A good lawyer, having seen x number of contracts over a year's time, knows a good deal and what the market will bear. You probably don't need a lawyer immediately but having a good one on call is very important if you want to be successful.

WHAT TO BRING TO AN IN-PERSON PITCH

Way too many songwriters have shown up with three briefcases full of tapes after I told them to bring their three best songs. The excuse is, "I wasn't sure what you like but hey, you're a nice guy—tell me what you think of this one, and then that one," until I almost have to resort to rudeness to make time for my next appointment. No one—REPEAT, no one—can listen to more than a few songs at any sitting and expect to remember a damn thing. Quick. Name the last five songs you heard on the radio. Was it in your home? Or car? Or office? Three songs could be one too many because there will always be one song that they'll like the least no matter how good all three are. It's apples and oranges.

Our musical tastes change as often as our tastes for food. Do you still listen to the same record you bought in high school day after day, night after night? Keep this in mind as you pitch your songs. If someone "kind of likes" a song, pitch it again six months later. By then he should be able to give you a more definitive answer. No two pitches are alike. The nice guy you met at a party on Saturday night can be cold and rude as hell on a Monday morning. If you don't get through the secretary after a try or two give it up for a week. You don't want to be announced as, "that so-and-so who's called twelve times this morning." Their time is as precious as yours and your reputation as a professional will be unproven. You don't want to be pushy and you don't want to be a pushover. It's a fine line.

Artist   *John Smith*

Label   *Dreadful Records*

Producer   *Tony Deaf*

Co-Producer   *none*

Manager   *Ron Decline*

Booking Agent   *Black Glove*

Attorney

Other Contact

Comments

Songs Pitched   **Date**

Here is an example of a simple form you can use to keep track of what you pitched to whom and when.

How you get paid

Your songwriting income will come from four sources: perform-ance, mechanical, synchronization, and print. Your performance royalties will come from your performance rights organization, your mechanicals from the record labels, and your synchronization from television and movie usage of your songs. The Harry Fox Agency, Copyright Management in Nashville, and other firms, are set up to negotiate these fees for you. They have a much better idea of what the going rates are than the average songwriter does. In a typical scenario someone will be performing one of your songs on network TV and you will be offered a "rate." Don't accept immedi-ately. These rates vary and you could be settling for much less than someone who has done their research could negotiate for.

There are stories still circulating around Music Row about songwriter/publishers who discovered one of their songs was being used for the grand finale of an already-filmed, multimillion dollar feature—and were able to get a very lucrative rate. It's not uncom-mon for you to be contacted after your material has been used. The book *This Business of Music* goes into depth about sync rights. Get a team of advisors you can rely on when the time comes for this type of negotiation. A good lawyer is a necessity when you start trying to read the various licenses you'll be asked to sign. Be careful.

The print rights to your songs can be another source of income. Once again it is in your best interest to research more than one print firm. *Billboard* lists the sheet music publishers of the hits in their weekly charts. These cover every style of music. John Bra-heny's book, *The Craft and Business of Songwriting,* also does an excellent job of discussing print deals.

The same things hold true for your monies from foreign coun-tries. You may at some time have to set up subpublishing deals over-seas and once again the right team of experts will make sure you receive your money. If you're starting to wish you could go back to your day job, don't panic. Your main priority should be to be a great songwriter. Don't let the business end get the best of you.

PERFORMANCE ROYALTIES

There are three performing rights organizations in this country: ASCAP (American Society of Composers, Authors, and Publishers); BMI (Broadcast Music Inc.); and SESAC (formerly known as the Society of European Symphony Authors & Composers). All collect performance royalties for their publisher and writer members. A publisher and a songwriter must both be affiliated with the same society for the society to collect performance royalties on their songs. So if you join BMI as a writer and want to work with another music publishing company, you'll have to find a BMI publisher. If you are an ASCAP writer and want to start your own publishing company, you'll have to affiliate your new company with ASCAP, etc. Of course, there are co-writing and copublishing situations where different people will be affiliated with different societies. It gets very complicated, and it's important for you to investigate what each society's rules are and what each has to offer. Each organization has offices in the major music centers and their representatives travel around the country appearing at various songwriter functions. Each organization does its job well and each one will be glad to tell you why they're better than the others.

Performance royalties are probably the biggest source of income for songwriters. Your song earns performance royalties whenever it is played in a concert, in a club, on a jukebox, on the radio, and in a nondramatic setting on television. It would be impossible for any songwriter to keep track of all those uses and then contact the parties involved and ask for payment. Fortunately, we don't have to, because performing rights societies do it for us.

Each performing rights society has its own formula for determining which songs are played the most often and consequently which songwriters and publishers get the biggest share of the royalty pot. Basically what happens is that they charge fees of all of the music users listed above. Then they calculate which songs are getting the most radio airplay and TV exposure. Based on those percentages, they split the royalties among all their members whose songs are being used.

Many songwriters who are caught up in the excitement of finally getting one of their songs recorded neglect to pay attention to the process of getting paid. Often an act will record one of your songs and even release it before all of the necessary paperwork is completed. Your performing rights organization will tabulate your performances and pay you by check quarterly but it usually takes at least two and a half quarters after the record's release for the first money to start to trickle in from BMI or ASCAP (SESAC is currently only one quarter behind). If you publish your songs yourself, you will be receiving a check for the publisher's share and another check for the songwriter's share of income from radio and television performances and other live performances. You will also receive a check on a less frequent basis for foreign royalties.

To get paid you must let the performing rights agency know about the recording by filling out a clearance form. This simple form will let them know the writer, publisher, title, artist, and release date. Something to keep in mind is that if your title can be abbreviated by those logging the song you may want to alert the performance rights agency's computer. Lewis Anderson's song "What Ever Happened to Old Fashioned Love," for example, was also reported back to BMI as "Old Fashioned Love." Lewis alerted them to this and found royalties that could have slipped through the cracks. Television performances may also be overlooked. Notify your performing rights agency when you know that one of your songs has been performed on a network TV show like "The Tonight Show" and doesn't show up on your statement for that quarter. The television network or the show's producer is supposed to furnish your performing rights agency with a cue sheet that will help them log your song. Once again, the song must be properly cleared and you should make a note on your own yearly calender just in case someone slips up.

When one of your songs is performed on national television or public radio make a note of the station, the date, the program, and the song that was used and inform your performing rights agency so that they can collect for you. They can't be everywhere, and sometimes you must look out for your own best interests.

As the publisher you will also collect fees from syndicated television shows for the use of your songs. These fees vary and will be negotiable according to the number of markets that the program will appear in. Ask questions before signing the initial license that they send you. It doesn't take much investigation to get a fair compensation. If the figures don't seem right it only takes one phone call to a collaborator or copublisher to see what they're being quoted. It's a long, slow process and the money seems to dribble in but as your catalog grows so will the number of profit-making copyrights.

The performing rights organizations are doing their best to collect your performance monies for you. You need to help them, though. With the staggering amount of music in use twenty-four hours a day it's easy for them to miss a song here and there. It's your duty to make sure that all songs that are recorded or about to be recorded are copyrighted and cleared so that the computers will be logging performances that will eventually translate into income for you.

Each performing rights society has its pros and cons and if you haven't yet affiliated I would suggest that you contact each and find the one where you feel the most at home. Talk to songwriters who are members and find out how they feel. Most of your income will be from performance royalties, and you don't want to wake up angry every day thinking that your collaborator at a different performing rights society is earning more than you. Get a feel for how each society logs airplay and TV performances and don't let the number of famous writer members at any one society impress you. Some songwriters change societies as often as they do publishers and this year's "star writer" may have been at the other society a year ago. All of the performing rights societies want to help you be as successful as possible and they are ready to answer most of your questions concerning publishing and payment for performances.

MECHANICAL ROYALTIES

You will be collecting money from the record labels on album and single sales but, alas, they too are always running a few quarters behind while your money draws interest for the label's bank account. An entire book could be written about payment nightmares from the major labels. A common example would be this.

John Smith, megastar, has recorded one of your songs. At the same time Jane Doe, megastar, wants to record the same song. You can't believe your good luck and politely inform Jane's manager that you would be honored to have her record your song but John Smith has recorded it and is promising a single. Time passes.

The label proceeds to pull four singles off John's current album but your song is not one of them. Jane Doe has had three top-ten records and didn't bother to record your song because of your up-and-coming John Smith record. More time passes.

In the latest issue of *Billboard* you see a full-page ad for John's record that states 500,000 copies of it have been sold, but when your royalty statement comes from the record label they are only paying you on 15,000 copies at the full agreed-upon rate. A few quarters later the label is still nowhere near paying you for 500,000 records and the statement says that they are paying at the reduced "record club" rate and that, in addition, there have been returns that are being applied against your account.

It's a no-win situation and usually there's not enough money involved to warrant an audit. It's easy to become very frustrated with the business side of the music business. I don't want to make it sound impossible because every day someone is getting his full amount due from the record label. But there's always the potential for problems.

I've talked about various trade magazines that you should read on a regular basis. When you have a record out pay close attention to interviews with the artist and the producer and even the label head. Every now and then, you find that someone is claiming in print that so-and-so has sold 100,000 records but your statement shows only a few thousand. Your research can pay off. Keep a clip file and try to find out how your songs are doing here and abroad. I have found reviews for singles I had out in Australia that my publisher never knew about. All of this may sound like a lot of paperwork and many songwriters prefer to leave the business end to a publisher (which is another reason why they never break away and step out on their own). But as you can see, you can really benefit by keeping on top of your songs' activity.

I'd like to believe that all of us will eventually get rich and famous from our endeavors but the sad truth is that unless you've got an A-side single by an artist that makes it to the top twenty, your earnings from performances and record sales will be meager. A songwriter/publisher can have twenty album cuts in his catalog and not make a thousand dollars a quarter. It's a real battle of survival when you consider that a demo of the song may have cost hundreds of dollars and you've also spent a considerable amount of money on your own equipment such as instruments, tape recorders, office supplies, etc. The slow cash flow has wiped out more new independent publishing companies than lack of talent.

Learn to look ahead. The adage about counting one's chickens before they are hatched really rings true in the music industry. I hate to think of how many times I've had the title song on an album by a best-selling group and never got the single. I've also had recordings by artists who had consistent label support until the release of my record. This could be partially due to the song but often as not the artist is refusing to cooperate with the label or the manager is a little too heavy-handed and somebody decides to "pull the rug" out from under the record. Hit records require teamwork and unless you've got everyone behind you all the way you won't make it up the charts. There's just too much talented competition.

COPUBLISHING

Imagine that you've pitched a song to a well-known act and they've recorded it. It's supposed to be their next single but you've spent all of your savings working as a publisher. How do you survive? Here are some viable alternatives.

If you can show that you can consistently produce songs as good as this one and are willing to give up a percentage of your publishing—normally 50 percent but sometimes 25—you might be able to secure a copublishing deal. In this type of situation you will retain a percentage of the publisher's share of the copyright and will probably be given some of the privileges that your new copublisher gives staff songwriters who have given up 100 percent of their publishing. These "perks" might include use of the copublisher's in-house studio and even an office space if he feels that he will gain by having you around. You will be part of a group of songwriters associated with that publisher, and when someone calls looking for songs because of another songwriter's good reputation one of your songs may go out.

A typical copublishing deal would take place like this: First, you will probably be asked to sign an exclusive contract for a period of time such as one year with a one year option (i.e., after the first year they have the right to renew for another year). You will be expected to continue to pitch your songs in conjunction with their staff and try to secure your own cover versions of your co-owned copyrights. The copublisher will give you access to his professional "pitching" staff. The tie-in to a major publisher will also help you expose your songs to the acts that he's been successful with in the past, as well as to your own contacts. It's a mutually beneficial situation if you can continue to create the same type of songs you did when you were writing for yourself.

Your copublisher's staff is there because of their ability to produce cover recordings. Take advantage of their services; they can help to give you even more time to write. This type of publishing situation will also usually include an office to work out of and an administration deal. It's a very tempting alternative once one reaches that level of the game. No two copublishing contracts are the same, though, and you should make sure that what you and your copublisher expect of one another is very clear. Make sure that you understand the renewal terms and that you know exactly what percentage of your copyright the copublisher will receive for their services. In copublishing deals the copublisher will usually retain a percentage of the copyright long after you have parted ways.

The disadvantages to copublishing deals are much like the disadvantages in a standard 50/50 publishing deal. Instead of writing songs for yourself you may find that you are trying to write the type of songs that the copublisher's song pluggers like best. As an example: You've always liked to write songs about trains, and when you bring in a new train song that you really like, the copublisher's song plugger doesn't even listen all the way through and gives you one of those "What-else-you-got-kid" looks. When you bring in a fifties-type song with a lyric that is almost too sweet to put your real name on he jumps up and down saying, "This is great! I didn't know you could write like this!"

It doesn't take long for a problem to develop if you start writing for the pluggers rather than for yourself. What's even worse is when they start to sell that type of song. I realize that all of us want to sell our songs and have hits but I'd hate to be expected to write the same type of song over and over again. It would be like being a painter whose dealer only wanted paintings of the same subject. You'd run out of new approaches after a while. It's a situation where you don't want to feel manipulated by your audience but you still want to remain successful. I hate to sound pessimistic. I know of many very successful copublishing situations and I know songwriters who have carried their catalogs from publisher to publisher looking for an ideal working situation. You just have to think about how a copublishing situation might affect your creativity, and about how much you are willing to compromise—or not.

This type of copublishing deal is generally available only to more established songwriters. The partners in these arrangements want to know that you're not going to need help developing your craft and that your catalog will constantly generate its own recordings. If you are a songwriter/artist and will be recording your own songs for a major label or even a smaller label with good distribution, you'll have a better chance of getting a copublishing deal. Publishers like songwriter/artists. There's very little work involved in pitching (because you record your own songs) and most of the covers will come from other artists buying the album and liking one of the songs.

I can't see writers giving up all of the publisher's share when they're going to be recording the songs themselves and there won't even be any demo expenses. But sometimes it's necessary, especially for beginners.

If you are setting out on a solo career (and are not interested in publishing or copublishing your own songs), seek out the best advice you can find before signing away all of your publishing. There are publishers who have been extremely beneficial in establishing new artists. They literally took these acts under their wing and served as manager/publisher until the acts were big enough to generate interest at the right level. They also introduced the acts to producers who worked with them in securing the best possible record deal, usually with a label they'd had strong ties to for years. Many acts have started out this way. The acts slowly acquired more share of the publishing as the years went by and their careers blossomed. If I were copublishing a songwriter/artist's catalog, I'd rather have 10 percent of someone who consistently goes top ten than nothing because we couldn't agree on a bigger percentage. (After all, all I was really doing was administering their catalog and mailing out checks.) Still, every day publishers let very successful songwriters go because they're "too demanding." I'm not for or against copublishing. The right team working your songs can provide the contacts and freedom from paperwork that you'll need to really be a successful writer. It's something to consider when and if your songs start to be recorded on a regular basis.

CO-WRITING WITH ARTISTS

If you're co-writing with a recording artist and don't already have a publisher you will probably be asked to put your part of the publishing share with the artist's publishing company or a company owned by their manager or record producer. Let's say that you've written three songs with an artist who has promised to record them for his next album. If no one asks for your publishing and you don't already have an established company with the performing rights agency, you should start your own and make sure that the artist's label knows that you should be contacted for the necessary licenses. If they want your publishing, it's not going to hurt to offer them half of the publisher's share. You have to at least try to negotiate. The artist will probably record the songs even without your part of the publishing. Too many writers give up all of their publisher's share in these situations because they assume it's "the right thing to do." The "right thing" will definitely win you new friends at the artist's publishers because you're signing away a share that's equal to what you'll receive! If you feel that you must give up all the publisher's share, at least get a good advance so that you won't have to wait for your money. Every copublishing deal is different and you can be very creative if you've got the right acts wanting your material.

A good attorney is essential in situations like this. Get someone who has experience in music publishing. Attorneys who don't have such experience usually aren't aware of current music industry trends. Seeking someone who handles this type of contract every day will really help in the long run.

ADMINISTRATION DEALS

Administration firms will allow you to keep 100 percent of your copyright and will usually require a fee that is a percentage of the song's total income. If their fee is 15 percent they'll take 15 percent from the writer and 15 percent from the publisher (which is 30 percent from you if you happen to be both). Nowadays there are many firms that will administer your songs for such a fee. The advantage to this type of deal is that you keep 100 percent of your copyright but you get someone else to do a lot of the time-consuming administrative duties of a publisher. This type of arrangement probably works best for a songwriter/recording artist who will be interested in getting his own royalties from the record label he records for and his performance royalties all collected at one central clearing house.

Some firms only handle collections and the paperwork necessary to make the collections, and other firms will actively attempt to secure other recordings of your songs and be able to get your material into motion pictures, etc. I have seen royalty statements from a number of these companies, and some are incredibly detailed accountings of every penny earned and what the sources were. Shopping around will be an education and you will probably want to contact your attorney again before you sign a contract with any of them.

As a publisher you will still need to supply an administration firm with all of the information about who's recording what and when it will be released. It doesn't hurt to make follow-up inquiries to make sure that once again your song didn't fall through the cracks. I can't recommend any one firm but you must remember that the bigger the roster, generally the less personal attention you'll get. Find out if the firm you're considering has someone who takes care of all of the clearances and copyright forms. If they have a local office near you, are those forms handled at that office, or will you have to make expensive calls to California or New York every time you want an answer? Ask about foreign representation and sheet music deals. If all that they're doing is opening your royalty checks and subtracting a fee you can do that yourself.

You need someone who sees the full potential of your copyrights. Do they get your songs into the song magazines I mentioned earlier? It's not really to *their* advantage to do so because there's very little financial remuneration from this type of publication. It's the exposure for *you* that's priceless.

If you're not prepared to do your own paperwork, an administrator can be of much assistance as long as you are ready to keep that person updated as to your needs. You need to be writing, demoing, and pitching songs, so try to create a situation that will be the least distracting to you on a daily basis. Ask for the names of some of the firm's clients the same way you might ask a plumber or contractor for references. It's an important decision and you won't feel like creating new material if you've got years to go on an administration contract that leaves a bad taste in your mouth. Will they offer you an advance? Does an outstanding advance affect the percentage they charge? What about tape copy costs if they also pitch songs for you? How are these items figured?

You'll need to investigate an administration deal carefully and, if you decide it's right for you, develop a good working relationship. You want their undivided attention but you also must give them time to do their job.

The relationship between a publisher and a writer goes beyond the written contract, and your administrator should be someone who you feel will pay attention to your needs. I once read about a president of a large manufacturing company who was looking for an advertising agency to handle his very lucrative account. The head honchos from the ad firm were ready to wine and dine him at some of New York's finest restaurants. Instead, he asked to go to dinner with the employees who'd be working on his account on a daily basis. His reasoning was that the president and the other higher-ups would only be available to him as he was about to sign on—or about to leave.

People are generally lazy. Make sure that the administrator knows how important your catalog and its exploitation is to you. This type of arrangement has been very successful for some writers and publishers so don't ignore this route. With the right partnership you should have all of the time you need to be writing, demoing, and pitching your songs.

WHEN TO CALL AN ADMINISTRATION FIRM

None of these companies will be very interested in working with you until you have already secured cover recordings of your songs that will make their percentage worth their time. One situation where an administrator would really be to your advantage is if a major artist hears one of your songs and wants to record it. Let's say that you've looked up the name of the artist's manager in a music business directory or on the back of an album and sent out a tape. The manager and artist love your song and plan to record it. The manager asks who the publisher is and, when you inform him that you publish it yourself, suggests that you let them have the publishing. This goes against your better judgment, but they also hint that you might get a single if they had the publisher's share. If you've never had a song cut you should be ready to start somewhere. Offer them half. If the song's that good they'll probably accept, and they'll also probably want to administer your half. But if the artist is significant enough, you can probably interest another administration firm in working with you and not give up that control to the manager. These are hard decisions to make. The more you read and learn about the music industry and what your options are, the better you'll be able to negotiate and make a decision that's right for you.

SEVEN

YOU'RE NOT ALONE

Much of the work you do as a songwriter and publisher is done in solitude. It's easy to feel isolated, but there are people you can work with and share ideas with.

COLLABORATORS

There will always be songwriters who only work alone and there are also songwriters who will only rarely collaborate with other writers. Most new songwriters start out writing by themselves and won't have collaborated unless they've been in a band or had an opportunity to meet other songwriters through seminars or workshops. A quick glance at the record charts or almost any album will show that most songs these days are co-written.

Choosing the proper co-writer is very important. You need to research your co-writer's abilities the same way that you would research a potential artist who might record one of your songs.

FINDING A COLLABORATOR

From time to time you might be in a local nightspot that features musicians and hear a performer whose musical style fits your own. After listening to the performance you can approach the performer and find out where he gets his material. In most cases you should already know (through your research) which songs were "cover tunes" and which were originals. Let the performer know that you're a songwriter and find out if he'd be receptive to listening to some of your songs. I've seen more than one singer who I first pitched songs to in some pizza place or bar become a well-known recording artist on a major label. Every singer likes to know that someone likes what he's doing musically. He also probably won't expect your songs to be very good so you have a chance to pleasantly surprise him. Don't be shy—if you like a fellow songwriter's work suggest that you try and get together sometime. It's easy to feel put off but sometimes songwriters will talk about collaboration for years before they ever actually get together. In a music center there are many possible collaborators and you need to choose wisely.

When you're first starting out you will write some songs that are almost recordable but need editing or a little professional polishing before you reach the point where you can successfully pitch them. Sometimes you'll have already spent too much money in the studio recording a demo version with a lyric that almost makes it and you become reluctant to make any more changes. But keep an open mind. If someone you respect makes suggestions that will obviously improve your song, don't hesitate. Follow the suggestions and if you can't make the necessary changes on your own, approach your potential collaborator and ask him what percentage of the song he'd like to help you finish it. Fifty percent of a good completed song is worth a lot more than 100 percent of a song that's unrecordable. Just make sure that you believe that the changes will improve the song.

No one should expect to be credited as a writer on a song for simply changing one line or word unless it radically improves it. Some producers, publishers, and recording artists have been known to add their own names as writers to songs that they've simply recorded. Personally, I think it's a crime and wouldn't allow anyone's name to appear underneath the title unless he or she has added a significant part to the finished song. If someone comes to you with a song already begun with another writer decide then and there how much work the song is going to need. If all the person has is a title and no lyric and you provide the entire lyric you may want to ask for more than just a third of the song. Generally speaking, if my name appears on a song with a co-writer I expect to receive 50 percent of the income from that song. I have been in situations where a collaborator put his initials next to every line that he came up with and started counting lines when we were finished with the first chorus. I was amazed at such a stupid waste of brain cells and never collaborated with that person again.

WORKING WITH A CO-WRITER
Once you start playing songs and learning each other's likes and dislikes it's relatively simple to start collaborating. There are a few

common pitfalls you should try to avoid.

Don't be timid. If you don't like where the song is going or what it's saying, SPEAK UP. Your name is going to be on the song along with your co-writer's, so make sure you believe in what it's trying to say. Some co-writers are very fast at writing lyrics and can intimidate you with how easy they make it seem. On the other hand, as long as you agree with what the lyric is saying let it stay. I've seen too many situations where songs were never finished because the writers argued over every word.

The trick to successful co-writing is the ability for two writers to create one voice that brings out the best in both writers. One of my better collaborators tends to write very melodic, pretty love songs that reviewers constantly refer to as "fluffy" or lightweight. I have often been accused of writing songs that have too cynical a viewpoint for the average listener. When this collaborator and I get together we balance out each other's weaker points. He's had some very "fluffy" songs go into the top ten and I've had many of my "cynical" songs recorded, but the songs we've written together are much stronger than many of the songs created on our own. I am a lyricist and have had to teach myself to write stronger melodies so I tend to look for a co-writer who may be weaker lyrically but who can "balance us out" with a strong melody. It will take a while, but once you learn your strong points you will be able to build up the confidence you need to collaborate.

Two heads are better than one in the business end of songwriting, too. There's the added advantage of having your co-writer also pitching the songs through his or her publisher or publishing company.

You're not married to any one collaborator. Avoid collaborators who get jealous when you write with others. Jealousy is a dead-end street and will only waste your time. Also, make sure the division of labor is equitable. If you come home from a collaboration session feeling like someone has been dumping all the work in your lap while he or she made coffee and took phone calls, finish what you've started and don't go back unless you have a song idea that only that person could help you write.

Avoid collaborators who have a negative viewpoint of the material. There are too many writers who write down to their audience, who figure on turning a quick buck with something "simple and stupid" for the rock and rollers or "dumb and hokey" for country music fans. Avoid them. They'll only slow your progress.

It's fun to work with songwriters who have been much more successful than you, but I know from experience that having a more famous songwriter as a collaborator doesn't guarantee that your song will ever be recorded. It all comes down to the individual song. It's a good feeling, though, to know that a songwriter you've admired from afar thinks enough of your talent to want to collaborate.

The great songwriting teams of the past—Rodgers and Hammerstein, the Gershwins, Harold Arlen and Johnny Mercer—can inspire you. Read some of their biographies to understand how magnificent collaborations work. A new book on collaboration is being written by Walter Carter, a frequent collaborator of mine. His book contract came about from our song collaborations.

Another unwritten rule: Always work with someone you feel you can learn from. There's a lot of give-and-take in any collaboration and you can learn a great deal from a good collaboration. The main rule is to write with someone who's going to work on the song as hard as you and be able to follow through once the song is done. Having an extra team "working" your song on the streets can't hurt either. You don't have to marry the person or become a confidante for all of his or her personal problems. All you need to do is believe that the two or even three of you can come up with a better song than you would on your own.

PROFESSIONAL ASSOCIATIONS

Trying to meet a fellow songwriter in a city or small town away from a major music center is a more difficult task. You may have to search and seek out like-minded musicians. There are songwriting groups in most of the big cities and often college towns will have a songwriter's association or folk music society. It only takes a small group of songwriters who want to share ideas and talent to start your own songwriter's group. It's an excellent way to find good demo singers or to meet other songwriters for collaboration.

Put some notices up at the local club where performers of the type of music you like appear. In some places the songwriters will come out of the woodwork. There may already be a songwriter's group in or near your town. Ask at local music and record stores or contact the Nashville Songwriters Association International (NSAI). They take calls from songwriters across the country and usually know of any songwriter associations near you. (And don't let the mention of "Nashville" lead you to believe that they only work with country writers. The seminars held by NSAI always feature songwriters, producers, and artists from every style of music.)

NARAS—the National Academy of Recording Arts and Sciences—offers membership to songwriters, musicians, producers, and others who have reached a certain level of success in the music industry. Once you become a member you are entitled to vote for the Grammy Awards, which they present. They also sponsor workshops and seminars for their members and the public.

In Los Angeles and New York there are ongoing workshops and support groups that are very helpful to songwriters at all levels. These come and go, so you will need to search them out the same way you would a record label or producer.

The Songwriters Guild of America is open to those writers who have shown some success in the field. The annual *Songwriter's Market* also has a list of organizations specifically aimed at songwriters. Get together with these groups and pool your talents to keep informed of opportunities to show your songs. The more you make others aware of your talents the sooner you will see results.

FROM SONG TO STORE

There's nothing like the feeling of finishing a great song. As a songwriter, you might feel like your work is over at that point. It's not. Your song is of no use to anyone if it just sits in your drawer or guitar case. After you've completed your song, well over a hundred different people will be needed to guide the song to the consumer. Each of these links in the chain needs to do his job properly for your song to be successful. There have been hit records that missed going all the way to the top only because half the radio stations in the country got the singles one week before the other half did. That one week difference caused enough confusion to slow the song down to where it never gathered momentum needed to reach number one.

Promoting a record is a long process and you want your song to get the attention it deserves every step of the way. Learn how it works. The salesperson at the local discount store is just as important as the bass player on the demo session. (The bass player's only encounter with your song may be for the few hours in the studio, but you can bet that if it's a hit he'll let the world know that he played on the demo!) There are many important people in marketing and promotion at record companies who may give your record an enormous boost. There are some very good books available on the inner workings of record labels that can also give you insights into all the people who will be involved with your record. Some music business career guides discuss many industry-related occupations.

Songwriters and publishers alike tend to be so tuned in to the workings of their part of the chain that they may not pay attention to what everyone else is doing. But the business is too competitive not to be aware of how the entire process works. You can start at either end and trace the path. If a discount store is carrying your song,

FROM SONG TO STORE

1. YOUR NEW SONG

2. PUBLISHING
Publisher's Secretary
Publisher or Assistant
Demo Musicians
Studio Engineer
Song Plugger

3. CONTACTS
Artist's Producer's Secretary
Producer
Artist's Personal Manager
Artist's Lawyer
Agent
Road Manager
Record Label

4. RECORDING
Artist
Studio Engineer
Master Musicians

5. LEGALITIES
Writer's Licensing Agency: BMI, ASCAP, SESAC
Record Label's Legal Department

6. IMAGE
Publicity People
Photographer
Record Label's Art Department

7. MANUFACTURING
Printing Company
Mastering Lab
Pressing Plant

8. SALES/DISTRIBUTION
Record Company Sales Reps
Local and National Distributors

9. DECISION MAKERS
Program Directors
Disk Jockeys
Record Promoters
Juke Box Suppliers
Record Store Buyers

10. CONSUMERS
Clerks
The Record-Buying Public

it's probably because their record buyer realized that the song was garnering chart activity. If you have a local hit record by a local artist, you can often influence the store buyer to stock your record. Have your family and friends ask for it. If the song is receiving radio play, some DJ or program director either chose the song himself or was alerted to the song by listeners calling in. Once again, family and friends can fan the fire.

HOW A RECORD EVOLVES

Let's follow a song along the path from conception to finished record. It's Monday morning and you've stayed up all night writing a new song called "Stayed Up All Night." You've been drinking coffee and playing your guitar and singing 'til you're hoarse and now you can't wait to get an appointment at your publisher's. (We'll assume that you plan to start your own publishing company in the near future.) You start calling at 9:30 and someone finally answers the phone at one minute 'til ten. The secretary can sense your excitement about your new song and promises to have the publisher or his assistant call you when he gets in. Unfortunately your publisher is in France at an international music convention and the assistant is going to be in the studio all day. It's now four o'clock and no one's gotten back to you. Hopefully, your initial excitement is still holding strong and you haven't edited the song to death trying to make it something that you know the assistant will like. Finally, you call back to the publisher's to learn why no one's called but the secretary does give you an appointment for Wednesday afternoon. You want to be prepared and know what to expect from this important meeting. Hopefully you've met with this publisher before (or know someone who has) and you know how polished they expect your demo to be before you play it for them. Some publishers and publisher's assistants simply *cannot* hear a song unless the demo has at least voice, a guitar, and harmony. They will not want to imagine how the drums sound and after playing them songs for a while you come to realize that they really need a demo that sounds almost like a record. With the advent of four- and eight-track home studios and the capabilities of computers this is no longer an impossibility. You (or you and some friends) should be able to come up with a work tape that has a more finished sound.

But for this appointment let's assume that "Stayed Up All Night" is such a great song that all you'll need is voice and guitar or voice and piano. Before your appointment the publisher's assistant gets a call for a bluesy uptempo song from a producer who's recorded songs he pitched him in the past. Just last year they had a top ten record on a song the publisher brought him and the publisher knows the producer will listen to anything he brings but he wants to bring something wonderful.

The appointment goes well and the publisher agrees that "Stayed Up" could be great, but he wants you to change the tempo and schedules a demo session with some live players for the following Tuesday. Your vocals won't fit the project so he leaves it up to you to find an appropriate singer while he has the secretary contact a guitar player, bass player, drummer, and keyboardist. You'll be playing rhythm guitar so you make a mental note to get some new strings at the local music store. The demo musicians are all in the union so contracts will have to be filed, but the secretary will handle all of that.

INTO THE STUDIO

The following Tuesday you arrive with your original work tape and enough cleanly typed lyrics for all the musicians plus the engineer. The publisher's assistant has changed hats and is now the demo producer. You and he have discussed the feel you're going for and you go into the studio to play rhythm guitar. Publishers will rarely demo one song at a time so you may have to wait while another songwriter's newest creation is demoed. If the other songwriter's song calls for a different instrument like fiddle or banjo there may be overdubs done right then or they may be added later.

Finally, the time has come and you play your song for the studio musicians who will write out a chart. Your home work tape will be played or you may perform the song on the guitar or piano.

For someone unfamiliar with the Nashville charting system it's a very strange experience. The leader of the session will call out "O.K. it's in D, 1145, 1145, 4455," and so on as you play the song through for them. Your chord pattern is being converted to a numerical code. The key the song is in becomes the number 1—1145 translates to D, D, G, A. In Los Angeles or New York the musicians will possibly have the music written out by an arranger in advance or else someone will do a "head" arrangement right there. The greatest advantage to the number system is that one can change keys in a matter of seconds. The numbers stay the same in B♭ as they would in D.

A lot of times the singer may be on a master session or busy somewhere else so you will have to sing a "scratch" vocal in a pre-decided key. Women and men sing in different keys. Always be sure the scratch vocal is done in a key that the hired singer can handle so that you don't have to search out another singer who can fit the track at the last minute. (If the demo's for a specific pitch to a certain artist you may want to go through that artist's albums and try to second-guess what key he or she seems to like to perform in. Many vocalists have a limited range and you want to create a demo they can sing along with.)

The demo goes down without any problems and you stick around while the keyboard player and lead guitarist embellish their parts. The engineer has another session elsewhere so you promise to meet later in the week to mix. You and the engineer will decide what part to feature when and will compensate for the volume you want certain instruments at.

Finally, almost a week later, you've got a mixed demo of "Stayed Up All Night." The publisher will keep the two-track master reel and make you a cassette to take home.

PITCHING THE DEMO

The song plugger loves the demo and promises to pitch it the following week. The song is now out of your hands. As a self-published writer you would have had to do both the secretary's and the song plugger's jobs. You would be the one making an appointment with the artist's producer and you would also be trying to get a copy of the song to the manager and the record label. If you live in a city with a concert facility where big acts perform, you can try to get a tape to the artist through the band or road manager. But I can tell you from firsthand experience that tapes pitched this way have a strong tendency to get lost before they ever get to where they were intended. I've heard stories of songs being pitched in restrooms but these were definitely lucky breaks and not common practices.

YOUR SONG ON HOLD

At long last you get word that all parties involved really think the song will work and you wait for the artist to come off the road so that he can hear it. Good news! The artist wants to record the song and it is now officially "on hold." This means that you won't submit the song to anyone else to record until the artist completes this recording session. Some acts are notorious for putting songs on hold for months and months. I really dislike that type of policy. Like anything else, there's an excitement that you transfer to your latest project, be it a song or a new car purchase, and that excitement will diminish as time goes by and you take on new songs and projects. If, after holding your song for months and months, the artist or group decides to bounce your song from the session for a song they just found, the excitement is no longer there. It can't be replaced. The song is now just an old song that so-and-so didn't record.

But that's not the case with "Stayed Up All Night." They've gone into the studio with a whole new set of master musicians who play on hit after hit. The producer, the engineer, and their assistants, plus an entourage of hangers-on ranging from the artist's attorney to the booking agent and bus driver, are all hoping for a smash so that they don't have to seek employment elsewhere. They've even got a string arranger and a quartet from the symphony to give it that special push in the bridge. All goes well again and the producer calls your publisher to come by next week and hear a rough mix.

At this point your publisher will copyright the song and work out the publishing agreements. If you aren't a staff songwriter they probably had you sign a contract with the company before they even did a demo. They asked you which performing rights agency you were affiliated with and made sure that the agency was notified and the proper papers were filled out. A license was also worked out with the record label and if they're a major publisher they undoubtedly have a collection agency (the Harry Fox Agency is one) to collect their mechanical royalties for them. The legal department at the record label will get the proper forms back to the publisher.

Meanwhile the label has listened to the new recordings the artist has done. A committee (that may include the label head and someone from promotion, the artist, and the producer) will choose the singles. Most albums will have three or four potential singles and these will be stickered on the album sleeve. The art department at the record label has been busy hiring photographers and everyone agrees that "Stayed Up All Night" would make a great album title. The artist flies in for a photo session. The tape of "Stayed Up All Night" has been mastered and the pressing plant is ready to stamp out singles. You've got the first single and they like the photo session so much that they plan to use an alternate photo for a picture sleeve. Finally, a release date is set and you mark your calendar.

PREMIUMS, PROMOTIONS—AND PACE

Back at the record label, the promotion department has decided to go all out. They've ordered alarm clocks for the control rooms of larger radio stations and coffee cups to send to the program directors at smaller radio markets bearing a new logo that reads "Stayed Up All Night." These premiums will also be sent to key record distributors and will also wind up as giveaways to buyers for major record chains and as in-store promotions. (You know the pitch: "Be the tenth caller and get a free album plus a coffee mug.") The local disk jockeys will be getting calls from the label's field people and, hopefully, the artist's fans will begin to request your song as soon as they hear it.

YOUR OWN BEST PROMOTER

There's a lot you can do to promote your own songs at this point. It only costs a quarter to write to the record label and let them know how much you like what an artist has recorded. If they're getting letters about the latest Fred Koller song, they may pay a little bit closer attention to the name when it comes time to pick the next single.

Let the radio people know how much you like your song (anonymously, of course). Radio listens to its listeners. If you think your song is a potential single, have your friends call the local station and request it off the album. You have to realize that many stations are on a very controlled format and can't play songs that the program director hasn't already chosen, but they will usually try to honor listener requests. The more they play your song the better chance it has to attract more listeners and hopefully more sales, leading toward a higher position on next week's chart.

Don't neglect the jukebox at your favorite restaurant or night-club. Ask and find out who services the machine and find out if they won't put your single on the box. Every little bit of effort will help expose your song to a wider audience.

The promotion staff will also be working hard to make sure that the record moves up the charts at the same pace across the country. You don't want to be number one in Maine and number forty-seven in Texas. You need points to climb the charts and thousands of calls will be made. Your hope is that jukebox suppliers and one-stop record distributors will get on the song early and start to get it into restaurants and smaller stores. The record store buyers for the major chains will probably not even consider carrying the record until it goes into the top twenty but you hope they will begin to get requests long before they actually have the record.

This also holds true of the local record store and your department-type stores like K-Mart and Wal-Mart. There is probably a regional buyer for the store but each one usually has a department head who will try to fill requests for product. By "requests," though, I am talking about albums or singles on major labels by artists already receiving airplay. No one can expect a buyer to go out and stock the store with an obscure single by an unknown band that isn't getting airplay already.

But if all goes well, then finally you, the songwriter, can go to the local store and the clerk has the hit recording "Stayed Up All Night" right there on the counter. I have been this route many times and it's great to go to a record store in a strange city and find recordings of my songs. It gives a great sense of accomplishment as both a songwriter and a publisher. I like seeing my name in small print on the record. I want the record-buying public to know that I was the creator of the song.

It's up to you to be your song's strongest supporter. I have seen some average songs do very well through a strong effort by the publisher and the artist's promotion team to break the record. Every airplay and sale means more income for you, the independent publisher.

Nine

THIRTEEN QUESTIONS

Much of your experience as a songwriter and/or publisher will be different from anyone else's. There's so much room for individuality, it's tough to spell out strict step-by-step guidelines. But here are some important questions commonly asked by the songwriters I meet at seminars.

Q: Would you please explain "copyright" in plain language?

A: It's easiest if I give an example.

You've stayed up all night with your guitar or piano and have a brand-new song to show to the rest of the world when they wake up. It may be written on a bag from the grocery store or on fine manuscript paper, but, essentially, what you have created is a copyrightable song that is the product of your mind. It's sometimes referred to as an "intellectual property." You own the melody and the words or, if you collaborated, at least a percentage of these parts of the song. When someone performs your song, or your song is recorded and sold as a record or printed and sold as sheet music, you, the copyright holder, have the right to collect income.

Your song is automatically protected by copyright law as soon as it is "fixed"—either written down or recorded on tape. It's important to understand copyright notification and registration. It's very professional to put notification of the copyright on your demos and lyric sheets. That would include the copyright symbol © or the word "copyright" or "copr." and the year and the copyright owner's name (it could be your name, your and your collaborator's names, or your publishing company's name). Even that, though, is not proof that your song is original, that you created it, and that you own it. If anyone ever takes you to court over these things, you will want to have your copyright registered. To register a copyright, you need to send $10, a Form PA, and a cassette or a lead sheet of your song to the Register of Copyrights, Library of Congress, Washington DC 20559. The phone number is (202)287-8700. Write to them for the Form PA and many other publications available on copyright. You can also copyright collections of your songs for one $10 fee, if you give the collection a title like "The Fred Koller Songbook." If after getting more information from the copyright office you're still confused, or if you think someone has infringed on your copyright, get a good copyright attorney.

Most songwriters and publishers don't go through the paperwork of registering a copyright until a song has been recorded or performed nationally. Once a song is recorded, though, it's required that you register a copyright and deposit two copies of the song with the Library of Congress. It's up to you to decide if you want to spend the ten dollars to register a copyright even before you start pitching your song, or if you trust those you'll be submitting songs to.

You will have total ownership and control of the copyright unless you sign over the publishing of your song to another publisher. Most publishers will ask for all of the publishing on a song. Think of your copyright like an artist's painting. When you sign it away, you are giving up the original artwork so that someone else can sell copies. The original painting or song now belongs to him. You assign your copyright to the publisher and you give him the right to sell it and exploit it as he sees fit. You'll receive all the writer's share of the song's royalties, and he'll receive all of the publisher's share (usually it's a 50/50 split of the song's total income).

In a copublishing deal, you may own a percentage of the publisher's share, but usually the other publishing company will still want to control the copyright. In an administration deal, you act as your own publisher so you own and control all of the copyright yourself. You just hire an administration firm to perform certain services for a percentage of the song's revenue (but you *don't* give up a percentage of copyright ownership in this case).

Q: What does it take to get your first song recorded?

A: I was extremely lucky and got a song recorded within the first month I was in Nashville. The artist who recorded the song gave me a small advance and also took the publisher's share of the copyright.

However, his recording of the song was never released and it was almost a year later before I got another song published. Eventually I was offered a staff position at a publishing company that was open to new talent and the rest is, I suppose, history.

No two songwriters start out the same way. In this business it's good to have a mentor who will answer the thousands of questions one has about every phase of the industry. Luckily there are many books now available for songwriters to learn from others' experiences.

Remember, there are no rules. No one can say that it can't be done a certain way. I have seen some songwriters become successful through some very strange routes.

I once pitched some songs to a songwriter/producer who had one of the cleverest ideas I've ever encountered. Most of us have stayed up late and watched "The Tonight Show" or the other late-night entertainments that run into the wee hours. I would also bet that most of us get another beer or run to the bathroom when the singer in the tight shiny dress who's opening in Vegas that weekend breaks into a version of "My Way." Not so for this guy. He would make a note of the singer and the song that she performed. The next day he would write a very polite fan letter raving about her performance. His logic, I assumed, was that if he could get his songs on "The Tonight Show," he would be a lot further along than many of us gave him credit for. He also figured that anyone who's working Vegas and the rest of the lounges of the world must make records, so he would pitch those artists his average country songs. From what I heard, he wound up producing albums on a number of these acts and got a lot of performance royalties from television.

I have another friend, a writer of novelty songs, who makes thousands of dollars every year from guitarist/comics who also appear late at night joking with the host and singing his songs.

Be creative. Create your own outlets. Every small town and city has some sort of celebration—a centennial, or heritage festival, or other event—that may require special music, and has a built-in audience. There's also the local church choir and high school loaded with local talent with lots of relatives to buy their records. I can see the ads now: "Vocalists Wanted. Should be from extremely large families; no experience necessary."

I've met a couple of songwriters who supported themselves with album projects based on historical facts that they turned into albums that were only available locally. It's also a great way to get studio experience, not to mention experience as the publisher/producer/songwriter and whatever else you choose to be.

There are grants available to those who qualify in many areas of the arts and humanities. I have also met songwriters who have used their own self-produced album as a master's thesis. Check it out. Leave no stone unturned (and all of those other proverbs that you haven't already turned into songs).

Q: What paperwork do I need to do if one of the songs I publish gets recorded?

A: Let's say your first song is about to be recorded. The producer and the artist both love it and plan to go into the studio. No one has asked you for any of the publishing and you're beginning to think that changing your last name to Gershwin wasn't that bad an idea. You wait for the phone to ring wondering if they'll know who to make the checks out to. Your friends ask you how much they're going to pay you to do your songs and you realize that you're not sure of the answer.

We've already discussed copyrighting your song with the forms provided by the copyright office. The next step is to affiliate with a performing rights agency, i.e., BMI, ASCAP, or SESAC (see Your Low-Budget Publishing Empire, Chapter Three, and Performance Royalties, Chapter Six). Once you've named your publishing company, you'll want to contact the label the artist records for. The label probably has someone who does nothing but contact publishers and get all the proper information, but if they don't contact you within a few weeks of the song being recorded, call them yourself. Records are released every day with "Publisher Unknown" beside the song title. The record company will ask you for a mechanical license and will send you their standard form. Have a knowledgeable attorney look over any license requests. They aren't that tricky, but some can be misleading.

You will have clearance forms to fill out for the performing rights agency so that they can pay you for performances. It also is good to make sure that the record label copy is correct. After all the work you've done you'll want them to at least spell your name right and have the correct publishing information.

If you do decide to go with an administrator or copublisher they'll probably be handling all of this for you, but it doesn't hurt to double-check and make sure that everything has been done. Eventually the royalties will head your way.

Q: How much music does a publisher have to know?

A: Do you own a guitar? Do you know someone who owns a guitar? If you can answer either question with a "yes" you have enough musical knowledge to be a publisher. I wish I had more of a musical background but all of my training is by "ear." I can play a blues or a country song with an interesting chord progression that uses the proper chords in the key of G, but that's after years of mistakes. Every time I sit down to play I learn something new.

The more music you expose yourself to the easier it will be. Don't close the door on a style of music just because you're unfamiliar with it. A former publisher of mine called one afternoon to tell me that he had heard "an English group" that he thought could do some of my songs. This was in 1983 or so and the group he was talking about—Dire Straits—had already recorded four or five albums. I politely agreed that yes, they certainly did have a vocalist that sounded like me but that as far as I knew all of their music was created by the group's leader. He sent a tape off anyway, but I remember walking around shaking my head, wondering why that particular publisher (a former record label head) hadn't been exposed to them before.

We can all be victims of that type of ignorance. There are hundreds of top black acts that I know nothing about; 99 percent of teenage America thinks that country music is Dolly Parton and Johnny Cash. If you want to break into a different style of music, study it. Don't pitch songs and make appointments if you don't know what you're trying to create.

Still, it's possible to spread yourself too thin. There's a great line in the movie "The Grey Fox" where they ask the leading man why he only robs trains. His answer was, "Professionals specialize." If you write great R&B lyrics, there's certainly nothing wrong with sticking with it and raising it to the highest level possible. Consider how you might scatter your talents trying to be a jack-of-all-trades.

There are studio musicians who also write songs and songwriters who are studio musicians, but the time you spend working on someone else's song is time you could be creating your own copyrights.

Q: Isn't it true that songwriters can sometimes get lost in the huge conglomerate publishers?

A: In 1973 I was signed to A.T.V. Music as a staff songwriter for a small weekly draw. We had a great little office and I worked with some wonderful people. While I was there I created over a hundred songs with other writers like Shel Silverstein, who's also a successful author. Soon I started to get some cover recordings. I would have gotten a larger advance if I'd been able to generate some hits, but even though I had more than one title that was recorded eight or nine times, none of them were hit singles.

A.T.V. and I parted ways but my catalog and copyrights remained behind. For a while they kept an office on Music Row and I was able to request tapes and still try to get a hit out of those songs. Then one day they closed the office and shipped everything off somewhere into limbo. The only way to even get a tape copy was to call their West Coast office, and that took a long time due to the size of the catalog they controlled. I had to inform them every time someone recorded one of my A.T.V. songs and royalty statements were late. For all I know I could have had huge international hits and never knew to collect the royalties. This does happen!

To make a long story longer, A.T.V. was purchased by Michael ("Bad") Jackson who let CBS Songs administer the catalog for him until SBK Entertainment World bought CBS. SBK is now my publishing representative for those songs. SBK already had thousands of copyrights and I'm sure that Fred Koller songs from 1975 that were never really hits aren't exactly a priority around there.

Sure, I could be pitching those songs myself, and there are some great titles in the collection, but I'm much too busy having number one records on the songs that I publish myself. The cost of hiring an attorney in order to get my songs back, not to mention the mental strife involved, makes it easier to write it off as another lesson in why you have to be more than a little bit crazy to continue in this business. I could be like many writers and quit right now saying that

A.T.V. got my best songs and CBS sold them to SBK, but just keeping that alphabet straight is more than enough work.

In retrospect, I should have tried to get a clause in my contract with A.T.V. prohibiting them from selling my songs without my consent, or having the copyrights revert back to me if they failed to hold up their end of the deal. But at the time I was so excited to actually have a "real" publisher that it never crossed my mind. And the attorneys I hired to review my contract told me that our agreement (without those clauses) was "standard." Slavery used to be "standard" in many states. I believe you get the picture.

Q: What should I do if someone wants my publishing share to record a song?

A: Imagine that you and someone you barely know have just co-written a song. She has a long track record and you've never had a song recorded. You agree that the song is a 50/50 split and each of you will split the demo cost. A demo is done and suddenly a major act puts the song on hold. The song was pitched by your co-writer's song plugger at the publishing company she is an exclusive writer for. Your co-writer never asked you what you intended to do with your share of the publishing but it would be unlike her to assume that you will give it to her employer. Don't be surprised if her publisher approaches you and asks for part of the publishing. It's in their best interest to see if it's available. If you really want to become a staff writer like your collaborator, now is the best time to cut a deal. But it's an equally good time to get your own company started. Some publishers may try to pressure you in this situation, leading you to believe that you will not be welcome around their offices if you don't play ball or hinting that the song "won't make the album" or be a single if they can't publish it. Call your attorney if these types of threats are made and he should be able to straighten things out right away. While you still control your share of the publishing, you have the right to refuse to grant a license on the first recording and that can certainly get their attention. Both you and the publishing company want this cut. This type of tactic is usually a bluff inspired by greed, and the fact that it's worked on uninformed songwriters thousands of times in the past doesn't mean you have to fall for it. If your co-writer was instrumental in getting the song cut, offer a percentage of your publishing share (one that you feel is fair), but don't give up all of it just because they ask you to. Let your lawyer get tough if you can't.

The best thing to do if you think there'll be a question is to talk it out with your co-writer first. If you work on a song with someone and you're not sure of the percentages, ask. They can and will vary. In most cases the split will be 50/50 between you and your collaborator unless otherwise specified. I have heard of "professional" writers who "charge" their beginning co-writers 25 percent to work with them but I find this despicable. If you both create something together you should share equally in the rewards.

Q: What do you mean by a song's "shelf life"?

A: A publisher expects each staff writer to turn in a certain number of songs a year. Many writers will have catalogs of well over a hundred songs at their publisher's. The publishers will also be acquiring songs on a song-by-song basis from various writers who are not on staff but still exchanging copyrights for advances or the promise of activity. At some of the larger publishers', it is not at all uncommon for the catalog to acquire a few thousand new songs every year. The major publishers are also actively acquiring other publishers' catalogs. These catalogs will usually contain a number of hits, some by writers who are still active in the music industry and a large back catalog of songs by writers no one's heard of (or from) in years. We're talking about a lot of good songs that nobody ever gets a chance to listen to. The staff writer's latest demos join this huge collection and will stay on top of the pile for only a brief period of time before they get buried by the other writers' newer demos. It's an endless cycle, and the song pluggers can't be blamed for not remembering a great song somebody gave to the publisher a few years back. As an independent songwriter, on the other hand, you have only your own songs to pitch and the shelf life phenomenon can actually work to your advantage. Here's how:

Your small but select catalog can be easily reviewed whenever you're not sure of what to pitch to certain acts. After you've been writing for a while, it's hard to remember every song you've ever written and it's wise to review your entire catalog on a monthly basis. Hopefully, your favorite song will be the one you wrote today, but that shouldn't make a song written years ago any less commercial. An unpublished song that's ten years old can become as contemporary as a song written yesterday with a new demo. Even songs written for specific artists can be re-demoed to appeal to someone else or quite possibly a new act has come along that is very much like the act you wrote the song for in the first place. Strive to write songs that will stand the test of time and be just as pitchable tomorrow as they are today. One of the reasons I believe that I have been able to survive as a songwriter is the fact that my older copyrights still get covered when I least expect them to. I know that if I wasn't constantly creating new songs and just tried to work the old catalog as strongly as I do the latest creations I would still be getting a steady number of covers.

A well-written song that has someone still believing in it and working it has an indefinite shelf life. Good songs can always be brought back out to a fresh generation of producers and artists. The main thing you want to strive for is to make sure that your demo or lyric doesn't sound dated. I have, on occasion, sat and listened while songwriters who got out of the business for a number of years took their old demos around looking for a new publishing deal. There's nothing worse than a dated-sounding demo.

There are already a number of books available on producing low-cost demos so I won't get into that area too much. The best tip that I have for you is to use the best musicians you can afford and always try to get four or five songs per session.

You may do two or three full production numbers with elaborate arrangements, but there's always time to have your singer (if you're not singing yourself) put down a simple voice and guitar or voice and piano demo of one or two songs. Often, this will be all that you need to get your song recorded. If the song is there it won't take an elaborate guitar solo to convince the producer that this is the hit he's been looking for. And a simple demo of this type is much less likely to sound dated a few years later.

Q: How often has someone tried to take one of your ideas?

A: The only situations that I personally know of where songwriters have had their ideas stolen were situations where unscrupulous publishers or producers, after listening to one writer's song about say, a blind dog, would ask their staff writers to bring in a song about a blind dog with one leg and a crippled schoolboy. The songwriter who was being ripped off couldn't really claim copyright infringement, but it was obvious to all parties involved except for the unsuspecting writers of the new song where the idea came from. Once you've put down your song in a studio, make sure that the dated bill has the titles of the songs demoed. This will help you establish a date of composition. When filling out contracts make sure that the date of creation is included. Lately, I've been writing most of my songs on a word processor that automatically records the date of composition. (Better living through technology.)

You can be paranoid and never play your songs for anyone, but the purpose of songwriting is to expose your music to as many listeners as possible. Worrying about song sharks and thieves does not serve your purpose. If you're suspicious of the people you're doing business with, leave. You are not a tree.

There are situations where publishers and artists will want to add their names on a song in which they've simply changed one or two words. To me, it's not worth it, no matter how big a star they are. I know of one famous writer who had one of his composition's melodic lines copied by another well-known songwriter. When asked about this infringement he said, "Well, at least I can sleep at night."

Titles are not copyrightable, and once one is established in a recording center, you will start to notice that many songs on the same subjects seem to appear simultaneously. There'll be a rash of songs about hands ("Daddy's Hands," "On the Other Hand," "The Right Left Hand," etc.). It may be related to the phases of the moon, or to some other phenomenon, but I'm sure that none of these writers were at the other writer's publishing company with a glass to the wall. Coincidences do occur.

If you hear that certain publishers or artists are involved in sleazy activities, don't play your songs for those publishers or artists! There's no gun to your head. You can be very selective about the people you offer your material to. If you really feel that you've been infringed upon, seek out a lawyer with experience in the copyright field. Unless the song that infringed on yours has become a big hit, it's probably not worth your time or money to pursue a lawsuit, but it never hurts to let those borrowing from your lyrics or melodies

95

know you've noticed some similarities. They probably won't try it again.

Songwriting should be a pleasure. I've known writers who were quite upset when record after record got dropped from someone's album at the last minute or a promised single was skipped over for a song that the producer published. Don't worry . . . if your material is strong enough another artist will come along and recognize it as a potential hit. As you pile up years of experience, your skills at creating songs will get better and better. Every songwriter and publisher dreams of the period when he gets "hot" and the world beats a path to his door. But it takes years of letting them know who and where you are before that happens.

This can be the most frustrating business you could choose, but it's also immensely rewarding. If you move to one of the major music centers, you'll be coming from a small pond where friends and family all tell you how great you are to a sprawling industry that's very jaded and slow to accept change. It takes awhile to get your foot in the door and your toes may get stepped on in the process. Your patience will be tested every day. It's a matter of learning to press on against all odds. If your songs are there, the rewards should follow.

Q: OK, so they aren't going to steal my song. I'm still paranoid. What do I do?

A: Here's a scenario: You've just invested a large amount of money on an expensive demo. You feel that your idea is fresh and original without sounding redundant, and you've come up with a musical "hook" that no one's ever thought of before. With all of these ideas ripe for the taking you send off a tape to a producer you've never met who is working with some of the best-selling acts in the country. Eight out of the ten songs on the last album by the artist you selected were published by his company but the last single was a song by a writer whose name you've never come across in your research. You hope the producer will be impressed with your creativity and cut your songs but you're still scared to death of being ripped off.

I've heard of situations where one artist heard another artist's album being mastered and was so impressed with one of the instrumentalists that he scrapped all of the solos on his album in production and hired that musician to replace those parts. His record came out first, and to the public the artist he was copying came out sounding like him! He didn't take the song or the title or anything else except the "sound" of the recording. You should expect a producer to "copy" your demo but you don't expect him to copy your production styles on songs other than yours and not give you credit. It's not really stealing but it's not exactly the way I would suggest a producer further his career.

In another situation that I've heard about, similar to the blind dog mentioned earlier, a producer/publisher receives a song called "Your Feets Too Cold," thinks it's a very clever idea, and summons his top writers. Over coffee, he suggests that the artist he's about to record needs some novelty material and that he has an idea called "Baby's Got Cold Feet." His staff writers unsuspectingly write a song that strongly resembles the unsolicited one. You really can't do much about this situation but call it to the publisher's attention that, like smoking, such activities can be dangerous to one's health.

I know many name songwriters who refuse to participate in seminars because they're scared that someone is going to claim that the name writer's big hit was an idea they were shown by a novice songwriter years before. I believe that these writers do exist, just like the con artists who deliberately fall down in supermarkets and sue for damages. At the same time I have heard songs with almost the same title and idea as mine from all around the country but they were each different enough that you'd know that the songwriters worked independently of one another.

People unknowingly lean on each other's melodies. We all tend to watch the same movies and look at the same books. I'm still amazed that Jackson Browne was the first to have a hit on the title "Tender is the Night." Some ideas are so obvious that it's embarrassing to say we missed the boat.

As I said earlier, you can't copyright a title. The Beatles' "Yesterday" wasn't the first hit with that title. Years after I had my first hit, "This Dream's on Me," I discovered a Harold Arlen song called "This Time the Dream's on Me" and a book by Dotson Rader called *The Dream's on Me*. Don't let paranoia stop the creative process. It's hurt too many songwriters. Your best song is your next song.

Q: I seem to write the same songs over and over. How can I break out of this rut?

A: Some songwriters become known for one type of song and are never considered for other recording projects. All of us have had strong musical influences and it's hard to hide them when we're first starting out. Nashville used to be crowded with bearded Kris Kristofferson-types who had very poetic songs and not much skill on guitar. They disappeared and were replaced with the John Prine clones who sang somewhat funny songs about getting stoned but never came close to his lyrical skills. I went through a phase where, vocally and melodically, my songs were reminiscent of Shel Silverstein's. Because of his influence on the pop group Dr. Hook, I have been told a few thousand times that my songs from that period were a lot like theirs and whenever I attempted to sing a demo, their name came up. I did write in Shel's style and our collaborations together are still songs that I am proud of, but I had a hard time developing my own identity—until I exposed myself to music that was totally different from any that I'd written before.

If you've never written on a keyboard, learn. If you play only quiet acoustic guitar, go out and buy or borrow an electric and write a song using its full potential. There are songwriters who buy or trade guitars a couple of times a year to get fresh sounds for inspiration. The different tonality of various instruments should trigger different lyrical and melodic ideas. There's no rut too deep to climb out of.

Finding a new collaborator can help. If your collaborators are boring, move on. Life is too short to be in a bad songwriting relationship. You don't need to have a fight or call a lawyer. Just move on. If you're meant to continue working together, at some point you will.

Q: Where can I look for inspiration?

A: I've already stated that the songs we hear on the radio aren't anyone's idea of how good songwriting could be and, from personal attendance at hundreds of songwriter's nights, I have come to believe that inspiration is equally hard to find wherever one lives. I am a lyricist and have always found that the more I read, the better the words are in my songs. I can see a definite improvement in the songs I'm currently writing from the songs I wrote a year ago. I realize that there are great songwriters who've never even read the cereal box at the breakfast table but I have always read for ideas. I have collected songwriter's biographies and recordings of songwriters performing their own biggest hits. Instant inspiration.

Some of us can go to a movie and come out inspired, or spend a rainy afternoon at a bookstore scanning the titles. Every one of those book titles was meant to "hook" you so you'd pick up the book and look inside. When your cassette is sitting on some producer's desk he's going to see your song title first. Your title should hook him in the same way a book title will.

Everyone has trouble staying inspired. For some unexplainable reason the staff writers at the large publishing houses frequently fall into a rut of all writing the same idea at the same time. You'll hear a song called "Dog's in Love," and then a week later "I Love Dogs," followed by a lot of songs about puppies. As an independent publishing and promoting your own songs, it's vital that you stay fresh and express a different point of view. Recently we've heard so many "back to the fifties" songs and small-town stories that it makes you wonder why the big cities are still so overcrowded. It's good to be topical but to be blatantly derivative is another matter. There are too many fresh ways to sing about a situation than to have to repeat what everyone else is saying.

Still, there will be times when nothing seems to work and you find yourself a victim of the dreadful writer's block. Or even worse, you find yourself unable to write but one kind of song. I spent a year writing painfully folky waltzes, so I know all too well what this syndrome feels like. Sometimes a new collaborator can help shake a slump but I often find that travelling to some town or city a couple of hundred miles away and sitting in an obscure diner or restaurant listening to the conversations around me will often help. Take a train trip. If you can't come up with a song idea on a train clacking into the night you might want to consider a career change.

The important thing is to stay enthused. The bigger an act, the higher the wall around them and the longer a line waiting to get in. You have to start with the lesser-known performers and then try to work your way up to the "inner circle." A really great song can make it a much briefer wait for success but all of us probably have a song or two that we really believe could be a standard if the world could only get to hear it. I am not a vocalist. I perform my songs, but only in a fashion to make the lyrics do all the work of entertaining the listener. I have written or co-written many songs that I can only present through someone else's version. I have successfully turned this obvious disadvantage around by writing songs that really grab the listener's ear lyrically and make him want to find out how the song will end. Whenever I've tried to perform songs that needed the melody to carry the listener I've felt a loss of contact and restlessness in the audience. I understand my weaknesses, so I understand why this happens.

I really believe that you should perform your songs in public as much as possible. In the first place, you never know who's going to be in the audience. I've gotten more than one song cut through a live presentation. Also, by performing live you develop a sense of what lines the public is really reacting to. The audience will let you know immediately if you're on the money. No waiting for a phone call from some producer. You can test a lot of songs in a night's performance.

Q: How do you deal with rejection?

A: You've purchased this book and followed every tip in it. Your record collection won't fit in a two-car garage and the local radio station is calling *you* for artist information. The tapes you're sending out are better than ever and you have made sure that everyone from the artist's mother on down has a copy of your latest creation. Still, new albums keep coming out and you haven't even had a song held. When you go through the album you find the usual mishmash of material that everyone agrees pales in comparison to your songs. You've invested enough money in home equipment to travel around the world and all you feel are doors being slammed in your face. It doesn't matter if you live in the middle of Music Row or in Timbuktu—these feelings of defeat will come around on a regular basis.

I know songwriters who have published some of the biggest hits of the last decade who still feel that it's impossible to get their songs listened to. Nobody said that it was going to be easy and nobody invited you to play. There are a lot of songwriters and only nine or ten spots per album. Most artists will also be songwriters and will repeatedly record their own songs unless the label or their producer keeps them doing outside material.

I guess that you do become accustomed to never knowing until you actually hold the record in your hands if your song's going to be recorded and released, but the waiting period can be a hard time when it's your first big recording by a known act. I've had title cuts that were never singles and singles that were never released and songs that have been recorded time after time and never made a single. There have been artists whose last record climbed into the top ten who have released one of my songs and never made the top fifty with it. It's a matter of luck, timing, and too many other factors totally beyond your control.

The only thing you can control is the quality of the original composition. There may be blacklists in some industries but I've never heard of anyone purposely not recording a certain songwriter's songs. The artist, or producer, or whoever made the decision just wasn't "hearing" your or my song on the day they were screening songs. Move on to another artist and make another pitch. What one of us believes is the greatest song of all time another will consider to be little more than sentimental drivel.

After fifteen years in this business I've also discovered that while I remain a songwriter plugging away at creating the best songs possible, the acts I pitched to ten years ago are for the most part barely remembered. Songs have a much longer lifespan than recording careers and the artists who do survive will come and go in the public's popularity. The labels they record for and the producers and management will also change on a regular basis. There are very few acts still working with the same team they were with even five years ago. If your song is as good as I would hope it would be, you can pitch it to a new set of ears. The artist may say, "I wanted to record that song back in _____ but so and so didn't like it. Let's give it a shot." There is also a strong possibility that due to the incredible amount of material one hears in a year's time, a person may have almost forgotten your song. Refreshing their memory will cause them to listen to it a little bit closer trying to remember where they heard it before.

Rejection probably accounts for more people giving up on the music business than any other factor. It isn't lack of talent, it's lack of recognition of one's talent that will do you in. Don't let them get you down. Learn to judge your career by how your own skills are improving. Even some of the biggest hits of our time were passed on by more artists than you would like to believe. But once again, every day there's some new artist just starting out looking for great songs. Familiarize yourself with the various songwriter magazines that feature interviews with songwriters. Time and again, they will have a sad tale to tell about "how long" it took to get discovered. I once heard songwriter Peter McCann talk about the various steps on the ladder to success. First it's "Who's Peter McCann?" Then "Get me Peter McCann." "Find someone who sounds like Peter Mc-Cann." And finally, "Who's Peter McCann?" Often as not, the time between each rung is only a matter of months. You need to stay busy writing and researching so that you don't notice the slow periods. Don't let rejection ruin your career.

Q: I'm leaving for Nashville soon—any more tips?

A: This is not a book on fashion, or how to dress for success, but time and time again I see new songwriters wandering around Music Row looking like the tourists that they are. They'll have planned five meetings for one day and will be carrying a briefcase with a cassette of every song they've ever written just in case the unsuspecting party screening songs happens to ask if they've got any songs about UFOs or blind newsboys. Surprisingly enough, you can play those songwriters a classic country hit and they'll say, "I got one that's better than that right here." Then they apologize for the demo which is usually a voice-piano rendition done by their great aunt. When you turn off their tape after a verse and a chorus they'll say, "The last verse is the part that's like that song you played me." It's a scenario that's repeated over and over again and it's no surprise that many of the parties responsible for finding material won't listen to outside songs in person.

There's no stigma to leaving a tape with someone and hoping for the best. I've gotten songs recorded by leaving a tape and so can you. Leaving a tape is highly recommended for the weak of heart. It can be painful to listen to a critique of your creation. Don't hurt yourself intentionally.

If you insist on being there when someone screens your material be prepared for the worst. Most of these folks don't care about your feelings or if the song is a true-life experience. They want Hits. Period. There aren't enough hours in the day to listen to all of the average songs being created by average writers everywhere. The person who's listening to your song is only human. For all you know his car wouldn't start and he didn't get that raise and you just came in from someplace he's never heard of demanding that your song be listened to and the receptionist has sent you back as a cruel joke. Don't jump up when he cuts off the first song halfway through the first line. Smile and act like it happens every day—you can rant and rave when you get home. Impress the person you're meeting with. Don't be impatient when the phone rings every five seconds. At least he's getting calls for material.

A good plan of attack would be to reconnoiter the area beforehand. Arrive a day or two early and find out where the offices are. If everyone you see going in and out is wearing a loud Hawaiian shirt you can probably leave your suit back at the hotel. Dressing like a contestant for a game show isn't necessary. If you're in Nashville you won't need to wear a cowboy hat to get an appointment. You may laugh, but I've seen some tacky homemade costumes in the waiting rooms of every label I've ever visited. Be professional and be yourself. If you wear a suit 330 days out of the year you shouldn't put on a western shirt to fit in. Your discomfort will show. Be relaxed. Nobody invited you, but that doesn't mean that you're not welcome.

TEN

A FEW CLOSING THOUGHTS

You have now had your own publishing company for a year or two and the royalties from a few initial records are starting to come in. Those first songs that you demoed when all of this was strange and new seem to be something that only archaeologists would be interested in. Don't fall into the same ruts that other publishers do and only work your newer creations. Make yourself review those first demos on a monthly, or at least a bimonthly basis. You may want to have a new singer you've had more success with re-sing some of the songs to either the original tracks or newer, more contemporary ones. You also may have gotten to know new contacts who should be made aware of these older songs.

THE DEMO SAMPLER

I rarely pitch more than one or two songs at a time but I have created samplers of my various songs that I really believed in for artists, producers, managers, and almost anyone else who's shown an interest in my songs. A typical sampler might be "Ten Female Songs from Fred Koller" or "Fred Koller Novelty Sampler." I update the Master sampler from time to time and use these tapes to refresh my own memory. It's impossible to predict what kind of song an artist is going to look for next. Artists are definitely as fickle as any of us. Often a song will travel with an artist for months or years before it's ever considered for recording. Sometimes an act will use one of your songs in their live concerts and still not record it for years. Those sampler tapes should always have information as to where to contact you and, if space allows, a listing of each song's writers. I don't care where someone learns about my song as long as they learn about it and give me and my co-writers the proper credit.

PITCHING YOUR OLDER SONGS

If you're a songwriter like myself with a number of catalogs scattered here and there it doesn't hurt to have whoever is administrating your old copyrights pull down the tape boxes and dig through some old songs that you still believe in. Often when you go by to pick up your tapes the comment will be, "You know, I never knew that such-and-such was even in this catalog. That's a great song for so-and-so. In fact, I sent a copy over yesterday." No publishing company that I know of has anyone actively going through his old copyrights on a daily basis. An enterprising song plugger could make a good career for himself by offering to dig out the gems in various catalogs for a share of the revenue generated from new recordings that wouldn't affect the copyright ownership. Unfortunately, most of the conglomerate publishers are sorely understaffed and can barely keep up with the writers already there.

Work your old catalog whenever time allows. A hit is a hit no matter how old or recent the song. The royalties will be the same for old songs as it is for new ones, and each new recording puts your name in the charts where you want producers to see it. No one will come to you looking for songs until you're getting so much activity that there won't be enough hours in the day to keep up. And even then, I would bet that publishers of your older songs won't even bother to dig around and see what they've got if you don't remind them. You have to create your own excitement by trying to stay in touch with former publishers if you want those songs worked after you've become an independent.

Don't be shy about giving tapes to those who request them. I'm as bad as the next writer about losing addresses and never following through when someone says they'd like a copy of this or that song, so I know first-hand that it's easy to slip up and not get a tape out. Once again, a ready-made sampler will give them something to listen to while you fill their requests for specific songs. I have gotten songs recorded by giving a tape to a friend who gave a copy to a friend and then on down the line, 'til finally it reached a recording artist who called me out of the blue to say that he'd just recorded one of my songs. It will certainly brighten up a gloomy winter afternoon to get that type of call. Many songwriters fear that someone will steal their song if they randomly scatter tapes across the country. By publishing yourself you should eliminate any contact with all of the songsharks and other shady types who want you to give them money for working your songs. Sure, there are crooks out there but being paranoid and not showing anyone your material isn't very productive. Keep your material out on the street.

FLEXIBILITY

If you live far away from a music center this may be the time to consider moving to one of the music capitals to try your luck. If you've already tried that route, it may be time to move away from the frustrations of constant rejection and go back and get your career focused again. Flexibility is what keeps the working songwriter sane. All because artist A passed on your latest song doesn't mean that artist D can't take it to the top.

The music business requires the patience of a saint and more than a little sense of humor. Its unpredictability is probably one of its strongest appeals. Every day is a crap shoot. As a publisher or songwriter you're like a fisherman with hundreds of lines being cast out again and again hoping for a bite. Songs that you wrote and forgot about decades ago can come back as your most popular copyrights. You can study an artist's career for years and years only to have him change record labels, producers, and hair styles all in the same week. If anyone claims he can predict what's going to happen next year or even next month, he's only kidding himself. Who could have predicted Tiny Tim? Even groups like Alabama sounded like every other bar band in America on their early recordings. Go with what your heart believes in. Pitch to performers you enjoy listening to who you believe will perform your songs with the same integrity with which they were written.

Keep your perspective. I have been in this business for only about fifteen years and I've already heard about too many suicides and heart attacks brought on by not knowing when to slow down. You can spend twenty-four hours a day in the studio or co-write in month-long marathons but this business can be very slow to reward you for a job well done. You've got to be able to believe in yourself and step back from time to time in an attempt to figure out where you are.

There will be times when you feel that you're in way over your head musically and there will be times when everything from John Philip Sousa to the Rolling Stones sounds the same. Learn to shift your focus when these feelings start to develop. There are times to retreat and regroup for your next attack. I know of songwriters who immerse themselves in foreign styles of music from time to time. After a while, subtle hints of these different styles will slip into their new compositions and recordings. As long as you don't lose sight of your goal (to get your songs recorded) it's perfectly fine to take diversions to stay fresh. Writing songs for the theater or a specific project could be all that you need to get back on track with a fresh new outlook. If all of your songs are waltzes try to write a blues number. Everyone falls into musical ruts from time to time and flexibility is a sure escape.

PERSISTENCE

One of the first things that happens when someone moves to a music center is he needs to write in isolation. He no longer performs in front of the public. The lack of income, coupled with the extremely talented competition that surrounds him, may make him soon wonder if he's really making progress. I've seen very talented musicians working in fast food restaurants just to stay in Nashville.

Don't work in a vacuum. The industry can take its own sweet time discovering you, and you need to be improving as a songwriter even if no one is recording your songs. One option might be to find an act that you could produce and develop using your talents and theirs in a team effort to get the music business to take ten minutes and pay attention. You can be researching the acts you wish would record your songs even if you haven't quite created the material you plan to pitch them yet. Wearing a lot of different hats should become second nature to you. Even after you've had chart success, you'll find you're only as "hot" as your last record.

A FEW CLOSING THOUGHTS

The number of songs published by independent companies that become successful chart records grows with every week's *Billboard*. In all styles of music the big-name publishing companies are no longer dominating the industry. Writer/producers who do most of their production work at home (aided by MIDI studios) have pop hits on a regular basis with a variety of artists. The industry is revolutionizing itself. With the new digital technology, the home studio will soon offer master-quality recording on a very limited budget. Producers are already asking songwriters and publishers for their backing tracks to use on their artists' recording releases.

If I were starting out today I would probably be learning to create records using as much of the latest equipment that I could afford. The multi-voice keyboards and drum machines available today make working with other musicians unnecessary. One can easily be a one-person band and create some wonderful music at home.

If you can create the songs, you can publish the songs. If the song is strong enough you should be able to get someone else to perform or record it. Once you figure out the proper outlets for your songs, your own creativity is the key to how successful you can be. If you've written a song for a certain type of act that's extremely successful but not open to outside material, wait awhile and offer it to the act that is challenging them for the audience. Once again, if your material is strong enough things should happen.

I have no personal battle with the major publishers. I wrote for a number of large publishing firms that have since been bought up by other firms who never pitch my old material. I played them my songs time and time again and realized that to write in that type of situation I would have to compromise my personal songwriting style. I wasn't the type of singer/songwriter they considered commercial and it was much easier for them to go with someone who was just like last year's model. I'm proud that my self-published songs get multiple covers and that songs many major publishers turned down or didn't "hear" have gone all the way to number one. I still find my own successes a little hard to believe, but hopefully every time an independent songwriter and publisher is successful it will make it a little bit easier for the next one of us to slip up the charts. If you can hang on financially and deal with the day-to-day frustrations of never knowing if you're still on course, you can eventually get your songs heard and recorded. Songwriting can become your main occupation if you work at it consistently every day, year after year. There may be "overnight successes," but they're few and far between. It's lots of hard work and very few rewards for a long time, but you will be building your own catalog that will improve with age like a fine wine.

The public wants new songs and new sounds. It's a dragon that won't stay fed. Its appetite is unpredictable so be bold, innovative, and most important, true to yourself.

I hope this book gives you some sense of what I do on a day-to-day basis and that you will adapt my approaches to those that work for you. No two songwriters achieved success the same way. There are no rules—that's one of the reasons it's such an exciting occupation. You never know who the next phone call will be from or what kind of new song you'll create next. I hope I'll get to meet some of you as I travel around the country performing and giving seminars. Good luck in all of your endeavors.

Gentle Reader—

By now you're hopefully ready to start pitching and promoting your songs to the artists you have carefully researched, and soon you'll be at a performance agency applying for your own publishing company. I wish you all the luck and patience you'll need and hope that you'll be extremely successful.

The fact that you can actually hold this book in your hands is still a miracle to me. I am and will remain a songwriter first, and the more slashes I add after my name the more confusing it gets. Songwriter/performer/publisher/author . . . with this many hats one can get confused from time to time. So on the advice of my attorney, please pardon a brief rejoinder. . .

I have done my best to give accurate information on self-publishing and starting your own business, however, I am not a lawyer. The laws of different states and countries vary, as will business procedures. I make no guarantees as to the completeness of any of the information in this book. It's your responsibility to check the information before relying on it. Neither I nor Writer's Digest Books can assume any responsibility for the information in this book or your use of it.

Best of Luck,

Fred Koller

INDEX

111